Endorsements for *Soul Nourishment: Satisfying Our Deep Longing for God*

"*Soul Nourishment* stirs the heart and whets the appetite of the soul to find God in deeper ways. Deborah Haddix sets before the reader a banquet of ways of engaging authentically with God. For the weary soul, this book will bring refreshing hope on the journey. With an uplifting voice of love, it opens a personal invitation for you to come and sit at the table with the Savior."

Susan Borgstrom, M.A.
Certified Christian Life Coach & Spiritual Director
Board Certified Christian Counselor

"There is nothing I long for more than to know God in a deeply rooted, life-changing way. But sometimes I need the reminder and encouragement to do just that. In *Soul Nourishment*, Deborah Haddix challenges us to pursue deep and intentional ways to nourish and care for our soul. No matter where you are in your spiritual walk, this book will deepen your craving to be more in awe of our Creator and allow that to permeate your everyday life."

Kim Young, M.A. Biblical Counseling
Classical Conversations Director

"Deborah Haddix's book, *Soul Nourishment*, offers words of encouragement for the crazy-busy woman. You will find creative, fun, and doable activities that will nourish your soul and fit you where you are right now!"

Mary Lou Caskey
Certified Christian Life Coach, Speaker and Blogger

"In her new book, *Soul Nourishment: Satisfying Our Deep Longing for God*, Deborah Haddix gracefully takes us through the spiritual practices we must cultivate to design our personal soul nourishment plan of action. Sprinkled with relevant and powerful Scripture, this book will guide you on a journey toward quality time with your Savior. And, if you're looking for resources to get you started, you won't find a more complete and comprehensive listing anywhere."

Kathy Bornarth, MA, LPC
Founder and president of The National Association of Christian Journal Writers,
Owner of Journaling4Faith and The Hope Counseling Center
www.nacjw.com and www.journaling4faith.com

"I have known Deborah Haddix as educator, ministry leader, and friend. Her heart is for each one of God's created beings to understand and know God to the very depth of our beings…to our soul. She gives us permission to look at creative ways in which to encounter the living God—to truly be changed, transformed. By gently guiding us to explore various types of journaling, praying methods, and studying of God's Word, we experience an authentic connection, which drives us to grow more, know more, and change more into the likeness of Jesus. Let the great adventure begin!"

Kari Glemaker
Assistant Director of Adult Discipleship
Hope Church

Soul Nourishment:
Satisfying Our Deep Longing for God

By Deborah Haddix

Warner Press, Inc.
Warner Press and "Warner Press" logo are trademarks of Warner Press, Inc.

Soul Nourishment: Satisfying Our Deep Longing for God
Copyright © 2018 by Deborah Haddix
All rights reserved.
Design & Layout © 2018 by Warner Press, Inc.

All Scripture quotations, unless otherwise indicated, are taken from The Holy Bible, English Standard Version. ESV® Permanent Text Edition® (2016). Copyright © 2001 by Crossway Bibles, a publishing ministry of Good News Publishers.

Scripture quotations marked NASB are taken from the New American Standard Bible®, © 1960, 1962, 1963, 1968, 1971, 1972, 1973, 1975, 1977, 1995 by The Lockman Foundation. Used by permission. (www.Lockman.org)

(NIV) - Holy Bible, New International Version®, NIV® Copyright © 1973, 1978, 1984, 2011 by Biblica, Inc.® Used by permission. All rights reserved worldwide.

(NIV1984) - Scripture taken from HOLY BIBLE, NEW INTERNATIONAL VERSION®. NIV®. Copyright © 1973, 1978, 1984 by International Bible Society. Used by permission of Zondervan Publishing House. All rights reserved.

Scripture quotations marked NKJV are taken from the New King James Version. Copyright © 1982 by Thomas Nelson, Inc. Used by permission. All rights reserved.

Scripture quotations marked (NLT) are taken from the Holy Bible, New Living Translation, copyright © 1996, 2004, 2007 by Tyndale House Foundation. Used by permission of Tyndale House Publishers, Inc., Carol Stream, Illinois 60188. All rights reserved.

The Message (MSG) Copyright © 1993, 1994, 1995, 1996, 2000, 2001, 2002 by Eugene H. Peterson.

All rights reserved. No part of this publication may be reproduced, stored in a retrieval system, or transmitted in any form or by any means—electronic, mechanical, photocopy, recording, or any other—except for brief quotations in printed reviews, without the prior permission of the publisher.

Requests for information should be sent to:
Warner Press Inc
2902 Enterprise Dr
P.O. Box 2499
Anderson, IN 46013
www.warnerpress.org

Editors: Karen Rhodes, Tammy Tilley
Designer: Curtis Corzine
Layout: Katie Miller

ISBN 978-1-68434-088-0
E Pub 978-1-68434-092-7
Printed in USA

DEDICATION
For every living soul

CONTENTS

Acknowledgments 11
Foreword 12
Introduction 13

PART 1

The Soul 17

1. Nourishing the Soul 21
2. Being Intentional with Our Soul 23
3. Pursuing Soul Nourishment 25
4. Listening to Our Soul 27
5. Spiritual Practices and Soul Nourishment 29
6. A Little Encouragement 33

PART 2

Spiritual Practices 37

7. Prayer 39
8. Engaging with Scripture 43
9. Solitude and Silence 45
10. Soul Searching 51
11. Soul Friendship 53
12. Simplicity 59

PART 3

Resources for Nourishing the Soul

Introduction to Resources 79

General Soul Nourishment Resources

1. A Check-up for Your Soul 82
2. Creating a Personal Sacred Space 83
3. Ways to Draw Closer to God 84
4. Nourish Your Soul A–Z 90
5. Ideas for Spending Time with God 91
6. The Ultimate Guide to Connecting with God 94
7. Ways to Feed Your Soul When You Are Busy with Life 103
8. Practice His Presence 105
9. Tips for Dealing with Distractions 110

Prayer Soul Nourishment Resources

10. How to Pray: A Biblical Guide to Prayer 114
11. How to Pray for the Soul 116
12. Tips for Praying Scripture 117
13. Pray Scripture 118
14. Praying in Color 120
15. Contemplative Prayer 121
16. Breath Prayers from Scripture 122
17. When You Just Can't Pray 123

Engaging with Scripture Soul Nourishment Resources

18. Ten Ways to Immerse Yourself in Scripture 126
19. Read the Bible with Focus 128
20. Bible Study Methods 129
21. Five Ways to Enhance Bible Study Time 131
22. Lectio Divina 133
23. Verse Mapping 135
24. Simple Bible Meditation for Complete Beginners 138
25. How to Meditate on God's Word 140
26. Biblical Reasons to Memorize Scripture 141
27. Tips for Memorizing Scripture 143
28. Scripture Memorization 144
29. A Method for Memorizing Longer Passages of Scripture 145
30. A Method for Memorizing Verses 146
31. Longer Passages for Scripture Memorization 147
32. Fifty Important Scripture to Memorize 148
33. "Soul" Verses (Partial List) 149
34. Soul Nourishment Scriptures (Partial List) 150

Solitude and Silence Soul Nourishment Resources

35. Tips for Enjoying a Time of Solitude 154
36. Extended Personal Communion with God (EPC) 156
37. Ways to Nourish Your Soul through Solitude and Silence 157

Soul Searching Soul Nourishment Resources

38. Questions for Searching the Soul 160
39. Questions for Reflecting on Your Life's Direction 161

40. Self-Reflection Questions by Category 163

41. A Daily Personal Audit. 165

Soul Friendship Soul Nourishment Resources

42. Cultivating a Soul Friendship 168

43. A Soul Friend is 169

44. Simple Ways to Show You Care 171

45. How to Encourage. 173

46. Twenty Things to Say to Encourage a Friend 174

47. Soul-building Words 175

48. Ways to Bless Friends Going Through a Difficult Time 176

49. The "One Anothers" 178

Simplicity Soul Nourishment Resources

50. Ways to Practice Surrender. 182

51. Celebrating the Christian Year 184

52. Ideas for Observing the Christian Calendar. 186

53. Christian Calendar Planning Form 194

54. Fasting 200

55. Fasting for Beginners 203

56. Tips for Engaging in the Spiritual Practice of Fasting 205

57. Scriptures for Fasting 206

58. Gratitude Scripture Challenge 210

59. Scripture Praise A–Z 211

60. Seventeen Attributes of God 214

61. My Father. 215

62. God's Words of Love. 216

63. God's Love for You 221

64. "In Christ:" What Does the Bible Say? 223

65. In Christ Jesus 226

66. My Identity in Jesus. 228

67. Oh, How He Loves Me. 231

68. One Word for One Year 233

69. One Word List of Possible Words. 234

70. Preach the Gospel to Yourself 237

71. Scripture for Preaching the Gospel to Yourself 239

72. The Spiritual Practice of Walking 242

Journaling Soul Nourishment Resources

73. The Benefits of Journaling 244
74. Some Journaling Ideas 246
75. Questions to Use When Journaling 247
76. Scripture Journaling 249
77. Topical Scripture Journaling 251
78. Possible Topics for Topical Scripture Journaling 253
79. Whole-Brain Journaling Techniques 254
80. Create 256

Open God's Love Letter to You! 258
For Further Reading 262

ACKNOWLEDGMENTS

I extend many heartfelt thanks to all those—family members, friends, and acquaintances who contributed to the making of this book.

Special thanks to my team—Peg Narloch, Barb Huff, Susan Borgstrom, Kim Young, and Karen Stringer. Your willingness to walk with me throughout this journey overwhelms me. Your commitment to detail, your constant words of affirmation and encouragement, and your faithfulness to "see it through" have been an inspiration. Thank you for proofing, providing input, and allowing me to bounce ideas off of you. You ARE soul friends.

Thank you to my husband, Don. Your love for our Savior and for me never ceases to amaze me. What an honor it is to do life with you. I treasure the privilege more and more with each passing day. Thank you for your words of encouragement and for your prayers during the research and writing of this book. Thank you, too, for the proddings, promptings, suggestions, and other input. And the fact that you went the extra mile by reminding me to take breaks, overlooking my negligent housekeeping, and "going with the flow" for dinner during this process was not unnoticed or unappreciated. I know by your words and actions that you are FOR me. I adore you!

FOREWORD

If you want to draw closer to God but aren't certain where to start, look no more. Deborah is a woman with a big heart for God and a passion for people to experience Him more fully. She has explored the countless ways humans can connect with their Sovereign Creator and compiled her insights into a one-stop soul nourishment reference manual.

There is no question that hearing from God and enjoying His presence comes through an intentional pursuit of Him. Deborah's book eliminates every excuse; the resource section alone is a gold mine of possibilities.

Nothing is more important than feeding your soul. Now you have not one, not two, but an entire smorgasbord of habits and practices to choose from. Each entrée yields a tantalizing and tasty treat.

Put an end to boring and stale devotional times now! Jazz it up with fresh ways to encounter God. Let this book move you into new and exciting ways to enjoy God and for God to enjoy you.

This book is waiting. God is waiting.
On your mark, get set, go!

Kinsey Oglesby
Heart Transformation Coach
Helping others hear God's voice and enjoy God's presence.
www.listeningtoabba.com

Introduction

*Bless the L<small>ORD</small>, O my soul, and all that is within me,
bless his holy name! Bless the L<small>ORD</small>, O my soul,
and forget not all his benefits.*

Psalm 103:1–2

Did you know you can talk to your soul? Take a look at Psalm 103:1–2 again. These verses tell us that David, a man after God's own heart, talked to his soul.

Your soul is a living entity. It has life and experiences levels of health. It needs to be nurtured—talked to, rested, fed.

For many years I lived under the premise that my soul was being adequately nourished by a traditional quiet time of Bible reading and prayer. And while there is absolutely nothing wrong with a traditional quiet time (sometimes it is exactly what our soul needs), my soul began to cry out within me that it needed more.

So, as I began to hear the cry of my soul and to acknowledge it, I actively began to listen to God speaking into my life…through the words of my pastor, Bible study discussions, the authors of books I was reading, the input of dear friends in the faith, and my own time spent with God and His Word. As I listened intentionally, I slowly started to understand there could be more.

While listening, I also heard over and over (Isn't that just how God works?) one particular message—we are God's image bearers and as such have been created uniquely by God Himself, the Supreme Creator of all. As His image bearers, we have been very purposefully wired. Perhaps, maybe just perhaps, the best way to commune with God, to nourish our soul, is to identify our unique wiring and discover ways to connect with Him through it.

And that is what I did. A few months ago, as spring was coming to an end and summer shone bright before me, I sat with God, my calendar, and my usual commitments. We were going to make a plan. The summer promised to be different than most. There would be much travel involved. Maybe signing up for organized weekly Bible study at church would not be the best idea this summer. A book study with a friend also did not seem the best choice. Both of these, activities I had spent the past four or five summers engaging in, had aided in my spiritual growth but required weekly participation. How could I be intentional about meeting with God in a way that would fit this unusual season of life?

So, throwing caution to the wind (at least that is how it seemed), I decided to do something entirely atypical for me. I gave myself permission to spend the coming summer on an exploration with my Heavenly Father. This was the summer to take what I had been discovering from my intentional listening and subsequent self-reflections and uncover some new "creative" ways to connect with Him.

For me, this has been a summer of fresh air and of much needed soul nourishment. A journey well worth taking—Illustrated Bible Journaling has created a fresh appreciation of His word. Squish-it journaling has evoked adoration and worship of His character. Praying in Color has drawn me closer to Him and helped strengthen my trust. Journibles have given me a way to see His Word afresh and promoted conversation with my Savior. It has been a summer to treasure.

Is the journey over? Absolutely not.

Do I love my Jesus more today than I did on June first? Oh, yes!

As I move from a life of spiritual mediocrity toward the full life He has promised me, do I desire more? Without a doubt.

And I pray that for you. I pray that you would not be content to settle for a life of mediocrity when He has promised you so much more—abundant life!

I pray also that as you begin to listen for the cries of your soul, this book would become a tool used by you to help you learn more about your soul and its health. I pray that in its pages you would discover ways to nourish your soul and to move toward the full life He has promised you.

PART 1
THE Soul

The Soul

An old story tells of two European gentlemen who set out on a quest to explore the heart of Africa. With native tribesmen serving as their guides, the men spent several days engrossed in the wonders of the land. Suddenly jarred by the calendar, a sense of urgency swept in. The explorers knew they only had a couple of days to return to port to catch the steamer home. If they missed the ship, it would be weeks before another one docked. In haste, they packed up camp and implored their guides to lead them back quickly. For two days the entire party moved along at a brisk pace. However, on the morning of the third day the tribesmen refused to move. Impatient to the point of agitation, the European gentlemen coaxed and prodded. Unaffected, the tribesmen remained unmoved. Their spokesman explained, "We have been moving too fast. We must stay here and wait for our souls to catch up with us."

I absolutely love this image. The tribesmen, responsible for leading those who did not know the way, steadily ascending the arduous mountains, and enduring extreme heat or continual rain as they climbed, suddenly came to a STOP—intentionally and deliberately, resting and waiting.

As I contemplate the Inca tribesmen, my thoughts turn to my own life. And the questions arise, "Just how often am I guilty of moving too fast? Do I, like the Inca tribesmen, understand the importance of stopping to care for my soul? Why does it need care? What exactly is a soul?"

It is not so easy to answer that last question. Even among scholars and theologians there are varying thoughts on the soul. Several articles can be read on the subject, in fact, and it is possible that each of those articles will offer a different opinion as to what the soul is. And each of these will be clearly supported with verses or passages from Scripture. In all honesty, the only conclusion to be drawn from such an endeavor is that a study of this nature requires the student examine everything carefully and in context.

Having said this, it is important that you understand this book is in no way intended to be a treatise on the soul. My purpose in putting this book together is to share with you (a busy woman with very little time on her hands) why caring for your soul is so important. I want to place ready-to-use, doable resources into your hands so when you close this book you can be about the business of nourishing your soul.

Let's begin with what we DO know about the soul.

First, the Word of God makes it clear that our soul is important. Our soul was created by God Himself (Jeremiah 38:16). It can be strong, or it can be unsteady (2 Peter 2:14). It can be lost, or it can be saved (James 1:21). Additionally, we know that the human soul needs atonement (Leviticus 17:11). And, we know it is the part of us that is purified and protected by the truth and the work of the Holy Spirit (1 Peter 1:22).

Next, we know that our soul is distinct. It is distinct from the heart (Deuteronomy 26:16), the spirit (Hebrews 4:12), and the mind (Matthew 22:37).

The soul is the essential personhood created by God AS YOU. It is the essence of humanity's being. It is who we are. Dallas Willard defined the soul as "the hidden or 'spiritual' side of a person. It includes an individual's thoughts and feelings, along with heart or will, with its intents and choices. It also includes an individual's bodily life and social relations, which, in their inner meaning and nature, are just as 'hidden' as the thoughts and feelings."[1]

The human soul is made up of three things:

- the will—our ability to choose
- the mind—our ability to think and reason
- the emotions—our ability to feel

Isn't it just like our God to create the soul with such complexity that even the experts cannot totally wrap their heads around it while allowing us just enough understanding for our benefit! I love the way John Ortberg defines the soul: "the coolest, eeriest, most mysterious, evocative, crucial, sacred, eternal, life-directing, fragile, indestructible, controversial, expensive dimension of your existence. Jesus said it's worth more than the world."[2] Doesn't that just say it all? Beyond our complete understanding, yet sacred and life-directing; fragile.

So, let's consider again what we DO know about our soul:

- Our soul is alive.
- Our soul is of great value.
- Our soul forms the very foundation of who we are.
- Our soul can thrive, or it can shrivel.

Our soul is like the silent, invisible yet necessary Central Processing Unit (CPU) of our person. "Our soul, and thus our soul's health, is the driving force behind everything that matters to us."[3]

Our soul lasts forever.

Think about it for a minute. Quiet your mind and think about your soul.

You have a living soul that lasts forever, and it forms the very foundation of who you are—it's incredible! But this forever-living foundation, this personhood of you needs care, for it can thrive or it can shrivel.

It is only through this understanding that we will see the need for our soul's nourishment. And once the need is seen, the question becomes, just how do we help our soul thrive rather than shrivel?

1.
Nourishing the Soul

Ultimately, caring for our souls is a matter of "nutrition." A soul that is lovingly and intentionally nourished will thrive. A neglected soul, one that receives little or no nourishment, will shrivel.

There are several contributing factors to the "shriveling of" or the "starving of" the soul. Here are just a few:

- busyness and the demands of everyday life
- exhaustion from meeting our many responsibilities and commitments to others
- under-valuing the importance of our interior life
- not learning the "how to" of feeding ourselves spiritually

These are things we can all fall victim to: preparing meals, carpooling, doctor's appointments, obligations to others, "I'll do it later," and on and on it goes. No one sets out to deteriorate the health of her own soul, but, it happens!

Some souls suffer from benign neglect, busyness and exhaustion causing their ill health. Other souls live on a starvation diet, lack of soul care knowledge resulting in their ailing health. All the while, these many suffering believers live in wonder of why they always seem so "hungry."

The truth is: the health of our soul matters! As the driving force behind everything that is significant to us, our soul's health is critical. Our soul requires tender, loving care in order to avoid shriveling.

Proverbs 4:23 says, *Keep your heart with all vigilance, for from it flow the springs of life.* The heart in this verse refers to our inner life; the soul. The verse teaches us, the springs of life flow from our souls; our CPUs. Let's think of it this way. The soul is a Stradivarius violin—the finest instrument, excellent, beyond compare. Massively expensive and unequalled, this Stradivarius still needs to be tuned because when it's left to itself, it constantly falls out of tune (just like our soul). When we keep our soul in tune, what comes from it is beautiful. When we fail to keep it in tune, the sound coming from it is deafening, offensive even.

What are some of those deafening, offensive sounds? Self-absorption, shame, apathy, toxic anger, physical fatigue, isolation, stronger temptation to sin, feelings of desperation, panic, insecurity, callousness, a judgmental attitude, cynicism, and lack of desire for God. When my soul has been neglected, whether benignly or through starvation, this is what tends to emerge.

Conversely, when we keep our soul tuned or nourished, the beautiful sounds of love, joy, compassion, giving and receiving grace, generosity of spirit, peace, ability to trust, discernment, humility, creativity, vision, balance, and focus emanate.

A healthy soul depends on a strong connection with God and receptivity to Him. Good theology, knowledge of Scripture, and days packed with good deeds for God do not necessarily equal strong intimacy with God. Knowledge of Scripture affects the mind, good deeds engage the emotions. Mere words or acts of goodness alone do not nourish the soul. The soul is nourished by God Himself. God must be found in personal experience—engaging, affecting, growing the mind, will, and emotions.

"Once we clearly acknowledge the soul, we can learn to hear its cries."[4]

You have a living soul, and it craves nourishment. Acknowledge it. Listen. What has your soul been crying for lately? Do you know?

How are you relating to your soul? What is that inner relationship like? When was the last time you made an intentional stop and thought about your soul?

Yearning for God is the very breath of our souls!

2.
Being Intentional
WITH OUR SOUL

*"We never draw closer to God when we just live life.
It takes deliberate pursuit and attentiveness."[5]*

Kathy Butryn

Nourishing our soul takes thoughtful planning.

The puritan writer, John Flavel, wrote that keeping our hearts (or souls) is our responsibility.[6]

If we want to find God, to nourish our souls amid all our "stuff," even good stuff, we must first DETERMINE to find Him. After this act of determination on our part, there must be the fashioning of a plan, one that is doable so we are able to follow through (Deuteronomy 32:47 teaches, *For it is no empty word for you, but your very life*).

Far too often our soul suffers from malnourishment because we have not planned thoughtfully. As you fashion your soul nourishment plan, be sure to consider your obligations and commitments, your priorities, and your God-gifted wiring. All of these contribute greatly to the success or failure of a plan. For example, we sometimes use the excuse that we are "too busy" to fit in time alone with God, but what we really mean is there are other things in our life with a higher priority. Personally, if I am honest with myself as I look at how I spend my time, I must admit I generally find the time to do the things I want to do. Fashioning a doable plan may mean sitting down with our schedule and our priorities and trimming out some of the fat—doing the hard work of reprioritizing, which might even mean removing some things entirely. It may even require cutting good activities to make time for better, necessary ones.

Along with being intentional about carving out time to nourish our souls, we must be intentional about learning to hear the cries of our soul. The voice of the soul can be difficult to hear because its cries come out sideways: through our emotions, our choices, our thoughts, our relationships, and even our bodies. Hearing our soul requires training. We must **learn** to hear it. And we can learn!

Margaret Feinberg makes the powerful statement, "God extends endless invitations to encounter Him, yet too often we sleep straight through. Unconscious of the life God wants for us, we slumber in the presence of the sacred and snore in the company of the divine."[7]

So how do we learn to hear those cries? Those invitations? How do we make ourselves more aware of God's presence with us and in us throughout our crazy, busy days? One way is to ask. Begin asking God today to help you be aware of His divine presence in your life. Then practice "noticing." Another way to become more aware of His presence and to nourish the soul is to engage in Spiritual Practices. (We will talk much more about Spiritual Practices throughout the book.)

Notice that it is all about intention and pursuit. Nurturing our soul and knowing God require action. Complacency is a deadly foe to our soul.

Oh, that we become believers with hungry, thirsting souls, pursuing an ongoing awareness of the living, active, Holy God who is crazy about us and has chosen to spend His days with us! May we be like King David who prays in Psalm 42:1–2: *As a deer pants for flowing streams, so pants my soul for you, O God. My soul thirsts for God, for the living God.*

3.
Pursuing Soul Nourishment

"I didn't say you should experience total contentment, joy and confidence in the remarkable adequacy of your competence or the amazingly successful circumstances of your life. It's total contentment, joy and confidence in your everyday experience of God. This alone is what makes a soul healthy. This is not your wife's job. It's not your elder's job. It's not your children's job. It's not your friend's job. It's your job."[8]

Dallas Willard to John Ortberg

We have within us the capacity to know God; the ability to know Him if we will but respond to His overtures.

Just as our physical body has physical eyes with which to see and physical ears with which to hear, so our soul has spiritual eyes with which to see and spiritual ears with which to hear. The problem for many is that often the sight and hearing of their soul has been dimmed by long disuse, or for some the dimming has been the result of unawareness. They have been uninformed regarding the presence of their spiritual eyes and ears. For others the dimming has occurred over time through unintended neglect.

No matter the cause, God never throws up His hands in exasperation with us. Never. Instead, He is patient. He is loving. Always in pursuit. Waiting, as Margaret Feinberg says, "for us to cup our hands in prayer and scrunch our faces against the vault of heaven in holy expectation that He will meet us in beautiful, mysterious ways."[9] That is His delight; that we come to Him, spend time with Him. And when we do our soul is nourished, and He brings to us the sharpest of sight and the most sensitive of hearing.

Some believers face an entirely different dilemma in the pursuit of soul nourishment. It is not that the eyes and ears of their soul have grown dim from disuse. Their love for God is firm. They serve Him. They spend time with Him. They, however, have somehow fallen into a soul-numbing rut.

We can faithfully observe a "quiet time," the discipline of which is helpful to us, but still find ourselves "hungry" in our souls. Perhaps the quiet time alone is not enough. If parts of our spiritual being are starving, maybe we need to expand our "menu" to include more balanced nutrition—spending time with Him in new and fresh ways.

Writer and pastor, John Ortberg, shares about a time when he was feeling quite ineffective and unhealthy in his soul. He decided to visit his long-time friend and mentor, Dallas Willard to seek some counsel.

> "I didn't say anything about having a quiet time," he gently corrected again. "People in church—including pastor—have been crushed with guilt over their failure at having a regular quiet time or daily devotions. And then, even when they do, they find it does not actually lead to a healthy soul. Your problem is not the first 15 minutes of the day. It's the next 23 hours and 45 minutes. You must arrange your days so that you are experiencing total contentment, joy and confidence in your everyday life with God."[10]

A.W. Tozer warns, "The whole transaction of religious conversion has been made mechanical and spiritless. We have almost forgotten that God is a person and, as such, can be cultivated as any person can."[11]

To have found God and still to pursue Him, that is the soul's paradox of love.

Consider Moses—Moses used the fact that he knew God as an argument for knowing Him better. *"Now therefore, if I have found favor in your sight, please show me now your ways, that I may know you in order to find favor in your sight"* (Exodus 33:13). From there Moses rose to make the daring request, *"Please show me your glory"* (Exodus 33:18). This same chapter in Exodus tells us that God was pleased by the passion and zeal of Moses.

4.
Listening to Our Soul

Once you are ready to begin intentionally listening to your soul, you might want to start in the book of Psalms. Within the pages of this book are many clues to what we should be listening for as we learn to listen to our soul.

In his article, "How to Care for Your Soul," Shawn Young lists some of the things that your soul may want to talk about:

> Psalm 42:2 reminds us that our soul needs to be refreshed by the presence of Holy God: "My soul thirsts for God, for the living God. When shall I come and appear before God?
>
> Psalm 63:5–8 informs us that our soul can be hungry: "My soul will be satisfied as with fat and rich food, and my mouth will praise you with joyful lips, when I remember you upon my bed, and meditate on you in the watches of the night; for you have been my help, and in the shadow of your wings I will sing for joy. My soul clings to you; your right hand upholds me." When Jesus said in John 6:35, "I am the bread of life; whoever comes to me shall not hunger," He was teaching His followers that they could satisfy their hungry souls with Him.
>
> Psalm 23:2–3 teaches that our soul needs rest: "He makes me lie down in green pastures. He leads me beside still waters. He restores my soul. He leads me in paths of righteousness for his name's sake." How do you rest your soul, or how CAN you rest your soul? What are your green pastures and still waters?
>
> Sometimes we are fearful and our soul needs refuge. Psalm 57:1-3 says, "Be merciful to me, O God, be merciful to me, for in you my soul takes refuge; in the shadow of your wings I will take refuge, till the storms of destruction pass by. I cry out to God Most High, to God who fulfills his purpose for me. He will send from heaven and save me; he will put to shame him who tramples on me. …God will send out his steadfast love and his faithfulness!"

Be attentive to times when your soul is overwhelmed with worries. Psalm 94:17-19 reminds us, *"If the* L*ord* *had not been my help, my soul would soon have lived in the land of silence. When I thought, 'My foot slips,' your steadfast love, O* L*ord* *, held me up. When the cares of my heart are many, your consolations cheer my soul."* God's Word is full of encouragement, reassurance, and tender words that your soul longs to hear. Meditating on God's promises is a powerful way to break the tyranny of worries.

Finally, listen for signals that your soul is distressed or suffering. Psalm 31:9–10 says, *"Be gracious to me, O* L*ord* *, for I am in distress; my eye is wasted from grief; my soul and my body also. For my life is spent with sorrow, and my years with sighing; my strength fails because of my iniquity, and my bones waste away."*[12]

5.
Spiritual Practices
AND SOUL NOURISHMENT

When we engage in spiritual practices (also known as spiritual disciplines), we are carving out time and space for paying attention to and responding to the ongoing work of God in our lives. By their very nature spiritual practices set us up for encounters with God. Spiritual practices can quiet our soul. They also help us to be open to the tremendous power and unfathomable love that is only available in God. Spiritual practices help us pull away from our day, sit down with God, quiet ourselves intentionally, and lean in to listen and receive from God. As we create this precious time and space with God, He moves to shape and heal, woo and nurture, correct and direct our inner being.

Simply put, practicing core spiritual disciplines helps us create plenty of space for God and, thereby, plays an extremely important part in the ongoing nourishment and health of our soul.

What exactly is a spiritual practice? A spiritual practice can be thought of as anything that is intentionally done with the purpose of helping one become open to and remain open to the ongoing work of God in her life. Spiritual practices are completely reliable ways of nourishing the soul and must be incorporated into our lives. There is no substitute. Spiritual practices or disciplines are not ways of earning merit. Neither are they an end in themselves. They are, rather, a means to an end: communion with God. They are wisdom and health to our soul.

Once we discover the value of spiritual practices to our soul's health, our initial response might be to search out a list of these practices that might direct us in the healthful nourishment of our soul; however, be advised that if you decide to go on such a search, there is no such thing as a complete list of spiritual practices. In *The Great Omission*, Dallas Willard defines spiritual discipline as "any activity that is in our power and enables us to achieve by grace what we cannot achieve by direct effort."[13] From this definition, you can see, that a complete list would be nearly, if not entirely, impossible to compile.

Willard, in another book, *The Spirit of the Disciplines,* gives us even more insight into this thing we call spiritual disciplines. In it, he says, "we call these 'spiritual disciplines,' but the activities are physical, not spiritual. So, a more accurate term is 'disciplines for a spiritual life in Christ.'"[14] (Romans 12:1–2 says *I appeal to you therefore, brothers, by the mercies of God, to present your bodies as a living sacrifice, holy and acceptable to God, which is your spiritual worship. Do not be conformed to this world, but be transformed by the renewal of your mind, that by testing you may discern what is the will of God, what is good and acceptable and perfect.*)

Discipline works by indirection. A discipline is something we can do that enables us to do what we have not yet been able to do by our own direct effort. "Trying" to engage in spiritual practices for the nourishment of our soul is not enough. We must "train" to engage in them. Paul tells Timothy in 1 Timothy 4:7 to *train [himself] for godliness.* Training connects us with a power much greater than our own—the Spirit of God that raised Jesus Christ from the dead!

Discipline also works because it helps us develop new and healthy habits, habits that engage our mind and heart with God.

There are two major categories of spiritual practices: practices of abstinence (self-denial) and practices of engagement (connecting relationally with God and others). Disciplines of abstinence make space for deeper engagement with God and others. Disciplines of engagement give strength to endure the challenges of abstinence. Using disciplines of one category without the other will not lead to much growth. To either improve or maintain our soul's health, we need to practice some tried and true disciplines from both major categories of discipline.

Some of the spiritual practices of abstinence are solitude, silence, fasting, and keeping a Sabbath. Spiritual practices of engagement can include Bible reading, prayer, journaling, worship, and self-reflection.

Jesus himself practiced spiritual disciplines. As we examine His earthly ministry as it is recorded in Scripture, we see that Jesus had exceedingly great responsibility and was certainly under more pressure than any of us has ever experienced. Yet Scripture verifies that he remained relaxed, patient, joyful, and generous with people—including many very difficult or very needy people. How did He do this?

The tendency is to brush this question aside by answering, "He was the Son of God." Yes, He was. That is a fact; however, it is not an adequate answer. Jesus was fully God, but he was also fully man, depending one hundred percent on the Indwelling Father.

The answer is that Jesus learned and grew in the context of his relationship with His Father. The learning and growing were a result of His abiding in the Father's love. His time with His Father was THE most important thing to him—not his ministry to others. Jesus sought out solitude, observed periods of silence, kept the Sabbath, and fasted. He also spent much time abiding in the Father's love through prayer, meditation on Scripture, fellowship, and worship.

If Jesus, the only perfect One, required "carved out" time with God, how much more do we?

6.
A Little Encouragement

My soul clings to you;
your right hand upholds me.

Psalm 63:8

....

As a deer pants for flowing streams, so pants my soul for you,
O God. My soul thirsts for God, for the living God.
When shall I come and appear before God?

Psalm 42:1-2

....

For God alone, O my soul, wait in silence,
for my hope is from him.

Psalm 62:5

Scripture says it all! Our souls LONG for God. Read Psalm 42:1-2 again. This is deep calling to deep.

God never moves into the human soul uninvited. We must learn ways to sit down, lean in, and pay attention to what God is doing in our lives. This is what spiritual practices help us do.

Learn, engage, lean in, and then delight in His presence. Taste and know the inner sweetness of God Himself in the very core and center of your heart.

Experience a glimpse of heaven right here on earth as the ears of your soul hear God speaking directly to you and as the eyes of your soul look out and meet the eyes of God looking in.

Spiritual Practices

I do not know your personal experience. It is quite possible that it has been very different from mine. Therefore, I will preface the following statement by saying that it comes from my own experience. With that said, I would like to share that it has been my observation that the standard advice in most churches when it comes to soul nourishment and spiritual growth is, "Read the Bible and pray." Now, while reading the Bible and praying ARE very good things, I believe this advice actually works for *very few* people. Many who receive this advice and strive to follow it actually end up feeling burdened when they fail to maintain consistency in the effort. And many give up.

In reality, the act of engaging in one singular spiritual discipline to the exclusion of the others rarely provides nourishment to the soul or elicits spiritual growth. The disciplines, remarkably, provide the most benefit to our souls when practiced in concert with one another. Speaking on the discipline of prayer, Dallas Willard (in *Spirit of Disciplines*, 252) once explained that in order for one to flourish in prayer, to develop an energetic praying life, they needed to practice it with other disciplines like solitude and fasting.

==The spiritual practices then—things such as prayer, Bible reading, solitude and silence, soul friendship, self-reflection, and simplicity—perform their best work in our souls when they are interwoven with one another.==

In this section we will take a closer look at a few of the spiritual practices. Please note that this is by no means a comprehensive list of the practices. These are what we might refer to as some of the core spiritual practices—practices that help us create time and space for God. And create this time and space we must!

There are far too many Christ-followers living lives of mediocrity. Too many who can identify with one young woman who, sometime after accepting Christ as her Savior, realized that she was not experiencing an intimate relationship with God. She was not growing in her faith, nothing in her life had even challenged her to come to God in question. Her busyness never allowed her time for rest or soul nourishment. The words, *"So that Christ may dwell in your hearts through faith—that you, being rooted and grounded in love"* (Ephesians 3:17), were merely that—words on a page of her Bible. They were not her personal experience. When finally faced with a season of darkness, this young woman sought help. Through a mentor, she was coached to abide in prayer, which allowed God to lead her toward an awareness of His abiding presence. She used Scripture to help focus her mind on God. She sat in silence, resting in His presence. Meditation and solitude were ways of exploring her heart. She "put on" the mind of Christ through worship and celebration; fasting taught her dependence on God. Practicing interrelated spiritual disciplines helped this young woman develop a life-habit of turning to God. It moved her from a life of mediocrity to God's promised life of fullness.

This is God's promise to each and every one of His children; a life of abundance, a life of fullness. He alone is our Creator, our Father, and He loves us passionately and perfectly! Why are we content to settle for mediocrity when we are promised so much more?

Make this the moment you aim for more than mediocrity: the instant you purpose to spend dedicated time nourishing your soul, the turning point in your relationship with your Heavenly Father. Begin by reading through the brief descriptions of the following core spiritual disciplines. Note how you might start implementing them into your daily life just as the young woman mentioned above did. Then explore the section of Resources toward the back of the book. Look for specific ways you can put these disciplines into practice beginning now.

I came that they may have life and have it abundantly.

John 10:10

7. Prayer

Prayer is simply conversing with God about what we are experiencing and about what, together with Him, we are doing. Prayer is a way of life. It is important that we think of prayer, not as mustering up energy and words, but as joining in with God's activity. Prayer is opening our lives to God and acknowledging our total dependence on Him.

By His grace, we have a compassionate Heavenly Father who hears our prayers and responds in perfect love for His glory and for our good. If that were not enough, we are assured in Scripture that God not only hears our prayers, He is waiting, expectantly, for them. *Before they call I will answer; while they are yet speaking I will hear* (Isaiah 65:24). That the Lord is attentive to the prayers of His children is one of the most encouraging promises found in Scripture (Psalm 18:6, 34:17, and 61:1–2).

These are breath-taking promises, yet many of us still struggle with prayer from time to time. The reasons for our struggles certainly vary, and there is no "one way" to turn things around. However, if or when you find yourself in a season of struggle in your life of prayer, you might find that one of the following ideas will help:

1. Give yourself permission to call out to God with an honest voice. For encouragement in doing so, simply spend some time in the Psalms. Throughout the book you will find prayers that are riddled with fear, anger, doubt, exhaustion, and confusion. Some time spent in the Psalms should convince you that it truly does not matter how "messy" or "dirty" your prayers are.

2. Be specific in your honesty. Thank God, who is the Source of all good things, for the blessings in your life; "name them one by one." Call out specifically anything you are worried about and ask for His help. Acknowledge areas of confusion and ask for wisdom. Feeling far from Him? Sit in silence; attentive to God's presence and love.

3. Train yourself to abide in prayer. To abide is to remain. To abide in prayer is to form a habit of resting in God's grace. When we practice Abiding Prayer, we are doing "soul work." There are several ways to teach yourself to abide in prayer.

> Search out short, meaningful verses or phrases from Scripture. Choose one and speak it/pray it several times during your day or marinate in the words for a day or so.

> Shoot up *arrow prayers*—"Jesus, teach me to pray. Holy Spirit, I rely on you. Lord, have mercy."

> Pray Scripture. Focus on the words in quiet prayer, slowly repeat them to yourself over and over, allow them to pierce your heart.

4. Use your imagination. God is the great Author, the great Creator. His Word is, therefore, full of wonderful pictorial images and illustrations. When praying Scripture, imagine it—run a video in your mind. The Biblical images can help you refocus when your mind wanders, and they can help you come to appreciate God's wisdom and grace.

5. Practice God's Presence. Try sitting alone in silence and solitude for five or so minutes at the beginning of your day. Settle yourself in God's presence before entering your day. Find a quiet spot in your home or possibly outside. Then during the day briefly return back to your time of quiet in God's presence as often as you remember (or set an alarm to help you remember). Developing this prayer habit will help you learn, little-by-little, *to pray without ceasing*, (1 Thessalonians 5:17) and to practice the presence of God.

6. Warm yourself up for prayer. Many people have trouble settling down for a time of prayer. Wandering minds, distractions, and restlessness among other things, plague the masses when it comes to prayer. Practice warming up for prayer by focusing on your bodily posture before God. It helps to engage your mind and heart on God when you are intentional about putting your body into your prayer.

7. Pray in conjunction with the practice of other disciplines such as solitude and fasting.

Prayer is a discipline of engagement. In its broadest sense of being conscious of God and relying upon the Holy Spirit, prayer is related to all of the disciplines for the spiritual life. It is a natural companion to solitude and silence, an indispensable confidant during self-reflection, and an innate companion to fasting.

Drawing close to Jesus is the only way to grow in prayer, and there is no better way to draw close to Jesus than to spend time with Him. Set aside a time of solitude with God; and pray. Observe a fast; and pray. It is through the practice of other disciplines that I find myself more and more in natural conversation with Jesus throughout the course of my day.

Another way to grow in prayer is to incorporate varying methods of prayer into our practice—methods that by their design, generate engagement. Consider Praying in Color, creating a Squish-it Journal, or taking a Prayer Walk. As these engaging practices become more habitual, stand back and watch. I am sure you will discover that you are carrying on many more natural conversations with Jesus as you wash the dishes or fold the laundry or even brush your teeth—all the while drawing closer and closer to Him.

Note that in order for prayer to become a way of living intimately with the Lord it must begin as a spiritual practice that then becomes habit. *But when you pray, go into your room and shut the door and pray to your Father who is in secret. And your Father who sees in secret will reward you* (Matthew 6:6). Do you see it? "When you pray…" Prayer must become an action that is "fixed" into our daily life. An action we do not even stop to think about. Scheduled periods of prayer are a necessary daily habit or discipline.

During His earthly ministry, Jesus had a *praying life*. He continually invoked God's presence in all that He did. Prayer lived in Him, even in His unconscious demeanor. And today, Jesus lives a *praying life* as He ever intercedes for us (Hebrews 7:25) and calls to us as He did to His disciples in the Garden of Gethsemane, "*Watch and pray*" (Matthew 26:41). Jesus is calling us! He is calling us into the conversation and activity of Heaven!

8.
Engaging with Scripture

Engaging with Scripture as a spiritual practice means to study, read, meditate on, be shaped by, and connect with the Person that Scripture proclaims. This practice includes the very familiar spiritual discipline of reading the Bible. It also includes study of the Word, memorization, meditation on Scripture, attending organized Bible study, praying God's Word, and the journaling of verses and passages along with many other ways of interacting with Holy Scripture.

Basically, this core discipline means to saturate your life with Scripture. Trust the Holy Spirit-inspired Word of Scripture as your guide, wisdom, and strength for life. Allow God's Word to wash your mind and restore your soul. Immerse yourself in it.

For the word of God is living and active, sharper than any two-edged sword, piercing to the division of soul and of spirit, of joints and of marrow, and discerning the thoughts and intentions of the heart.

Hebrews 4:12

....

Let the word of Christ dwell in you richly.

Colossians 3:16

Jesus Himself lived by Scripture. It was His guide and nourishment for life. His life was saturated with Scripture. Jesus spent large amounts of time interacting deeply with Scripture in a variety of ways. He read, studied, memorized, meditated on, and prayed the words of God.

Time. Depth. Variety. Jesus went far beyond using a daily quiet time. And because He saturated Himself with God's words over the course of His lifetime, these words provided His life's mission statement, strengthened Him to resist Satan's temptations, taught Him to compose the Lord's Prayer, inspired His wisdom to develop and live out the Sermon on the Mount, informed Him about the cross, and helped Him to endure the cross (and all His trials). It was His intimacy with God's words that also empowered Him to overcome by the love of the Father and the power of the Spirit.

Employing oneself with Scripture is the most fundamental discipline of engagement. All of the other disciplines for connecting with God are assisted when we, at the same time, are interacting with Scripture.

For example, engaging with Scripture and solitude complement and strengthen one another when they are paired. These paired disciplines are a prime example of the relationship between the disciplines of engagement and abstinence. Praying Scripture gives us strength both to endure and to benefit from solitude. Solitude, in turn, makes "soul space" so that we are able to absorb Scripture, particularly when we devote hours to being alone and quiet before the Word of God.

We can rely on Scripture, take comfort in it, be corrected by it, find hope in it, and receive direction through it.

If your soul is crying out for engagement with God's Word but you are unsure how to begin, take some time to look over the Engaging with Scripture resources provided in the final section of this book. In the resources that have been compiled, you will find several suggestions—some traditional, some more creative—for nourishing your soul through time spent with the Word of God.

9.
Solitude and Silence

Solitude

Solitude as a spiritual practice is the intentional refrain from interacting with other people in order to be alone with God. It is a hard discipline to practice, but one that is essential to the well-being of our soul. Oswald Chambers explains, "Solitude with God repairs the damage done by the fret and noise and clamour of the world."[15]

To be effective, solitude must be practiced in conjunction with silence, and the two are absolutely basic to the nourishment of our soul. We practice solitude and silence by finding ways to be alone; away from talk and from noise. These are disciplines of abstinence. We rest, we observe, we "smell the roses," we do NOTHING. And *that* is the most important aspect of solitude and silence—doing nothing! This is not a time for production. It is a time to focus on intimacy with Jesus—a time to attend to the Lord alone!

This discipline of combined solitude and silence can also be used of God as a means of grace. In this posture of rest, of doing NOTHING, of attending to the Lord alone, we may be blessed to experience the awe of our salvation, the wonder of being justified by His redeeming power. And in these moments, we realize our status with God is not by any DOING of our own—not by our strivings or by our achievements, but by His grace!

Solitude—unplugging, experiencing God as He restores our soul—is one of the most important of the spiritual disciplines. Solitude, in fact, is a life-giving discipline. It fulfills our soul's deep need and is necessary to its health. We are designed for time spent in the quiet, simply being with our heavenly Father.

As we use it here, solitude means EXTENDED time alone with God. Interestingly, in his book, *An Unhurried Life,* Alan Fadling uses this very meaning to rename solitude. Fadling chooses to refer to the discipline as Extended Personal Communion with God,[16] reasoning that this term sounds warmer and more inviting to him than the word solitude. Perhaps a renaming will be helpful to you also as you seek to make periods of solitude a regular part of your soul's nourishment.

Of course, God is always with us and certainly, we all experience short periods of alone time with God. Solitude, however, is an intentionally planned period of at least two hours and upwards of several days. It is a time of focus on God and our relationship with Him. In drawing aside for lengthy periods of time, we seek to rid ourselves of the "deterioration" of soul that results from constant interaction with others and the world around us. In this place of quiet communion, we are able to discover again that we *do* have a soul and that it needs to be nurtured. It is here in this place that we begin to experience the presence of God in the inner sanctuary, speaking to and interacting with us. And it is here that we understand once again that God will not compete for our attention.

We must arrange time for our communion with Him as we draw aside in solitude and silence. This precious time will not just happen. We must be intentional in scheduling it. The psalmist said, *"Cease striving and know that I am God"* (Psalm 46:10, NASB). *Cease.* End. Stop. Deliberately come away from the striving. Make the time.

Striving. God's provision for us is adequate. His work through us is adequate. It is not our responsibility to make anything happen. It is essential that we stop shouldering the burden of "outcomes." Every outcome is completely and safely in His hands. There is no need for striving.

One of the most common responses to the suggestion of practicing extended times of solitude and silence is, "I don't have time! I have too much to do." The truth is you do not have time *not* to practice solitude and silence. No time is more profitably spent than that used to heighten the quality of an intimate walk with God. When through practice (and it takes practice), you learn to withdraw from everything in your life in order to seek the Lord alone and find your sufficiency and joy in him, you will see your life change dramatically! Your intimacy with Jesus will become the secret epicenter of strength in your heart.

Remember that God never gives anyone too much to do. We do that to ourselves or allow others to do it to us. And all too often we allow ourselves to get in that "too busy" state because the things being presented to us are "good things!" For those who see themselves as too busy with good things, it is important to point out here that it has been said, and insightfully so, "The greatest threat to devotion to Christ is service for Christ." Allowing service for Christ to steal our devotion to Christ is a fundamental failure in the nourishment of our soul. Being too busy for Christ is no excuse. No matter the reason, through our busyness we are still robbed of valuable time with Him and our very soul suffers. We can, however, be delivered from busyness through the deliberate practice of communing with Christ in times of solitude and silence. Our soul can receive essential nourishment, and God's power can be actively and wisely sought and received, enabling us to grow by grace into Christlikeness. The result of this deliberate soul nourishment?

Power, with Christ-like character.

In *The Spirit of the Disciplines*, Dallas Willard shared what one young Christian who had been guided into the effective practice of solitude and silence had to say:

> "The more I practice this discipline, the more I appreciate the strength of silence. The less I become skeptical and judgmental, the more I learn to accept the things I didn't like about others, and the more I accept them as uniquely created in the image of God. The less I talk, the fuller are words spoken at an appropriate time. The more I value others, the more I serve them in small ways, and the more I enjoy and celebrate my life. The more I celebrate, the more I realize that God has been giving me wonderful things in my life, and the less I worry about my future. I will accept and enjoy what God is continuously giving to me. I think I am beginning to really enjoy God."[17]

Where is a good place to get alone for an extended time with God? If you have a weekend or a couple of days to devote to such an experience, schedule a visit to a retreat center, hotel, cabin in the woods, or your favorite beach. If you only have a few hours, pack up your tote and head out to a nearby park, coffee shop, restaurant (during a slow period), or church sanctuary. You might even observe a time of solitude and silence at home by getting up early one morning, sending the children to Grandma's, or spreading a blanket out in the yard on a beautiful afternoon or under the stars.

Jesus practiced solitude and silence.

> *And rising very early in the morning, while it was still dark, he departed and went out to a desolate place, and there he prayed* (Mark 1:35).

> *But he would withdraw to desolate places and pray* (Luke 5:16).

> *Perceiving then that they were about to come and take him by force to make him king, Jesus withdrew again to the mountain by himself* (John 6:15).

These are just a few of the verses that show us the pattern Jesus had of going into solitude and silence. Practicing solitude and silence is an important way that Jesus fostered His intimacy with the Father, from which He heard His voice and was empowered for His ministry. He taught this same practice to His disciples.

And he said to them, "Come away by yourselves to a desolate place and rest a while." For many were coming and going, and they had no leisure even to eat. And they went away in the boat to a desolate place by themselves (Mark 6:31–32).

"Come to me, all who labor and are heavy laden, and I will give you rest. Take my yoke upon you, and learn from me, for I am gentle and lowly in heart, and you will find rest for your souls. For my yoke is easy, and my burden is light" (Matthew 11:28–30).

Demands of daily life make it difficult to really hear from God even when you have scheduled the intentional time away to do just that. Before settling into your time of solitude and silence, take the time to turn off all electronics. If you are at a coffee shop or restaurant that is full of hustle and bustle (or streaming music), pull out your ear buds and use them to block the sound. Be deliberate in setting yourself up to pay attention to God.

In the beginning, your time of solitude might be a bit rough. Again, go into it prepared. Not only might you have to battle to focus your mind, but you may have to war with your body. This foreign time of quiet and stillness is likely to feel unpleasant to your body as it goes through withdrawal from all the things that have been activating and exciting you. Think this through ahead of time. Prepare ways to make your body more comfortable without getting so comfortable that you fall asleep.

Take some time today, or at least in the next week, to practice this incredible and powerful discipline of solitude. As you do, be patient with yourself and with God. In the discomfort of the silence, continue to sit. Allow the quiet and emptiness that surrounds you to be filled with His presence. Sit right there across from him. Climb into his arms. Enjoy deep communion. He longs to be with you.

Madeleine L'Engle describes it this way, "Deepest communion with God is beyond words, on the other side of silence."[18] Yes, silence is uncomfortable, but deep communion is indescribable. Be intentional. Be persistent in solitude and through it experience deep communion with your Heavenly Father—a communion where words are not required.

Silence

Silence as a spiritual discipline is the practice of drawing away to a quiet place and not speaking so that one might quiet her mind and whole self in order to attend to God's presence. During silence we abstain from sound in order to make space for a deeper engagement with God and with other people. This means that silence is also the practice of refraining from speech during conversation with others so that we can truly listen and be a blessing to them. In our culture silence is rare. There is no quiet space. No time to listen to God. No time for personal reflection and prayer. But in God's Word we see that silence is essential.

> *But the Lord is in his holy temple; let all the earth keep silence before him (Habakkuk 2:20).*

> *For thus said the Lord God, the Holy One of Israel, "In returning and rest you shall be saved; in quietness and in trust shall be your strength" (Isaiah 30:15).*

> *"Be still, and know that I am God" (Psalm 46:10).*

In 1 Kings 19:12 the Lord showed Elijah and us that to sense His presence and hear His message we need to be quiet and listen for *the sound of a low whisper* of the Holy Spirit.

To be quiet enough to listen for "the sound of a low whisper" is very difficult for most of us. We are not comfortable with silence. We squirm in the hushed stillness after a question has been asked or fidget during a lull in conversation.

Another difficulty many of us experience during times of silence is that most of us do not know how to handle the distractions that break our concentration. To be silent requires practice. It begins with training our minds and bodies to be fully present to the Lord who is fully present to us.

Begin slowly, ever so gently. Start by spending five minutes in silence with God. Set your kitchen timer or an alarm on your phone and just sit with God. When your mind wanders, acknowledge it, and bring your focus back to listening.

Or practice being quiet in your mind as you read Scripture. Pause on a verse. Be still and slow down your thoughts. Savor a word or phrase. Reflect on God's words to you. Linger and listen to the Lord. Just stop reading, quietly absorb, and simply rest in the loving arms of Christ. Take a "Selah"—a pause to reflect and pray; a sacred space to be still and quiet before the Lord; abiding in His presence.

Implement either of these suggestions as you begin to observe times of silence with the Lord or choose one of the suggestions from the Resources Section of this book. Begin with baby bites if necessary, but by all means begin today to nourish your soul with the sustenance of solitude and silence.

10.
Soul Searching

We all have "stuff!" Our "stuff" might be fear or anger or bitterness. It might be pride or selfishness or worry. It could actually be any number of things. The Bible calls our "stuff" sin. This sin that we continue to carry around gets in the way of our growing relationship with God and contributes to our soul's ill health.

Soul-searching or personal reflection is the spiritual practice of paying attention to our "stuff" in order that we might grow in our love for God and others. Soul searching is very important to the health of our soul. This practice helps to reveal our "stuff"—those things that draw us away from God.

Searching the soul is not an easy task. It is, in fact, a very difficult and humbling experience—one that causes us to realize that we are not as wonderful as we think we are and that life is simply not all about us. Soul-searching can even at times be an extremely painful experience.

Engaging in periods of personal self-reflection helps us to learn more about ourselves than we ever knew before; hard things—things we wish we did not know, things we do not want to admit to ourselves, and especially not to others, things that need to be acknowledged and dealt with.

The spiritual practice of soul-searching *IS* hard, but the benefits of the discomfort and, yes, even the pain are so worth it. It is through recognizing, acknowledging, and releasing to God these very hard, personal things that we are drawn closer to Him. It is here where we discover that God has given us a greater purpose; a purpose for His glorification and kingdom advancement, not a purpose that revolves around us. It is here where we learn to live our lives by God's design.

Search me, O God, and know my heart! Try me and know my thoughts!
And see if there be any grievous way in me, and lead me in the way everlasting!
Psalm 139:23–24

There are some thoughtful questions in the Resource Section of this book that you might choose to work through as an exercise in self-reflection. As you read through the questions, commit to answering them honestly even if the truth is hard. Take some time. Do not hurry through this task. You might even choose to record your answers in a self-reflection journal. This added element will provide you with information for future soul-searching and become a written record of your spiritual journey.

11.
Soul Friendship

Soul Friendship is the spiritual practice of engaging fellow disciples of Jesus in prayerful conversation or other spiritual practices. It is an intimate, life-giving relationship that helps you pay attention to the activity of God in your life and helps you to respond.

A soul friend is a friend who knows your history, who knows your weaknesses, who celebrates your strengths, and who knows God intimately. Margaret Feinberg says, "Often God places people in our paths who spark internal joy simply by being themselves."[19] These are the people who can become cherished soul friends.

The relationship between Jonathan and David provides us with a wonderful, biblical example of soul friendship. *The soul of Jonathan was knit to the soul of David, and Jonathan loved him as his own soul* (1 Samuel 18:1). That is a powerful bond. It is clear from this verse that Jonathan did not perform any work of his own in order to knit his soul to the soul of David, but that God absolutely showed up in that very moment to forever knit their hearts and souls together. God knew something at that moment—the moment of knitting—that neither Jonathan nor David could have envisioned. He knew just how much they would need each other in the years and events to come. God brought them together at a point in their lives when He knew each would serve to make the other a stronger man than either of them would be alone.

Soul-knitting is not for the faint of heart. Having your soul knit to another means you bear your own hurts right along with those of your friend. Soul-knitting is putting your heart and your name in the hands of another person and saying to them, "I trust you with all of this; with all of me." And it is having that person do the same with you.

Much like soul-searching, engaging in soul friendship can be hard, but the benefits are so worth the time and effort. Soul friends love harder, laugh louder, live richer, and become more together than they could ever be on their own.

A soul friendship can be one of God's greatest gifts to us. God's essence is community, and He designed us in His image—the image of community. We have been designed as highly relational beings. Yet, many of us struggle and are even fearful when it comes to entering into this type of friendship. So why do we resist intimacy with others?

Simply stated, we resist because our deepest wounds and our greatest trauma in life stems from relationships. When we become wounded at our point of connection with others, we become wounded at the very core of our identity.

It is only through a deep, close relationship with our Heavenly Father that we can bring ourselves into this type of friendship. In his book, *Connecting*, Larry Crabb states:

> Releasing the power of God through our lives into the hearts and souls of others requires that we both understand and enter into a kind of relating that only the gospel makes possible. This kind of relating depends entirely on deep fellowship with Christ and then spills over on to other people with the power to change their lives, not always on our timetable or in the ways we expect but as the sovereign Spirit moves.[20]

The potential power of the Holy Spirit being poured into another person's heart and soul depends on our own deep fellowship with Christ.

Ordinary friendships are built on intimacy, trust, and mutual enjoyment of one another. Soul friendships share these same qualities but are also characterized by an additional element. Soul friends actively help each other pay attention to God. This additional element is what makes these friendships so powerful (Ephesians 4:16). When we are struggling, soul friendships can still connect us to God.

In the Resources Section, you will find resources on what to look for in a soul friend and how to go about cultivating a soul friendship. The marks of a spiritual friendship are honesty, self-awareness, genuine love and acceptance, openness, and authenticity. Another mark of a spiritual friendship is that this friendship is "agenda free." There is no "plan," no "what can I get out of this" on the hearts or minds of either friend. Quite the opposite. In a spiritual friendship we are concerned for the well-being of our friend. We want them to "win." We are FOR them!

Two key ideas regarding spiritual friendship emerge for us from Henri Nouwen's insightful words:

> "We have probably wondered in our many lonesome moments if there is one corner in this competitive, demanding world where it is safe to be relaxed, to expose ourselves to someone else, and to give unconditionally. It might be very small and hidden. But if this corner exists, it called for a search through the complexities of our human relationships in order to find it."[21]

When it comes to spiritual friendships there is the need for safety and the need for a search. Each of us longs to find a safe place to be ourselves, to let down our guard, to be accepted and loved for who we really are. But, the truth is, we will most likely have to search intensely in order to find it.

Being aware of what makes relationships "safe" in the way Nouwen described can go a long way in helping us develop soul friendships. Henry Cloud and John Townsend offer three hallmark qualities of a safe person in their book *Safe People*:

1. Safe people draw you close to God. Safe people understand your dependence on God. They gently draw you in the direction of receiving what you can and must from God directly. They encourage your spiritual development, are quick to remind you that God cares, and that He is at work. They, also, encourage your full surrender and participation in whatever God might ask of you.

2. Safe people draw you close to others. Safe friends will not try to isolate you from your other important relationships. They are FOR your marriage, your work relationships, and your friendships beyond themselves. When appropriate, they gently push you towards resolving conflicts rather than merely allowing you to vent your frustration.

3. Safe people draw you close to your true self. This is perhaps one of the most difficult qualities to observe, yet one of the most powerful when working correctly. A true, safe friend can see where you are stuck and also see your potential—and they join the fight for your soul's freedom from the barriers.[22]

Once we have established a soul friendship, there will be times when we invite another quality, mirroring, from this friend whose perspective we trust. Mirroring is when our spiritual friend acts as our "mirror." There are times when our friend is able to see things in us that we cannot see ourselves. Sometimes our friend will even lovingly take the risk to venture an unsolicited observation in the hope that it will stimulate growth and life in us. Many times, soul friends are the ones who call out in us gifts and dreams we barely know are there. Sometimes, though, they call out the darker themes like fear, resentment, and hopelessness.

As we said before, soul friendships can have messy, hard moments. Since these are the friendships where trust has been formed and vulnerability established, difficult truths about ourselves will have to be faced from time to time. Even though there is an unspoken vow that soul friends will do their best to never cause each other pain, it can happen (or at least be a bit uncomfortable).

Not only might we feel pain in hearing hard things about ourselves, in the depth and authenticity of our friendship, we may have to hear hard things about our friend. She could share difficult things about herself. So difficult that even though we deeply, truly love her, our initial response might lean toward one of two particularly unhelpful, even destructive, extremes.

First, we may be tempted to recoil in horror at what she has shared. When someone finally comes to the point of "coming clean," we often cannot believe what we are hearing, and it shows. Honestly, we would rather not hear it. We do not want that to be the truth about our very seemingly together friend. Often, in this situation we go to the place of horror or shock. Instead, what we want to be is "present" with them. Be present in a way that receives their confession as a fellow struggler—which we very much are—who deeply respects their choice to bring their darkness into the light. Thank them for sharing. We can genuinely do this for each other, even when we have no earthly idea what else to say. Thank them for being willing to entrust to you this essential ingredient in their own development. Encourage them, reminding them that exposure is the key first step toward freedom.

When a struggle is exposed or a sin confessed, we know that in the unseen world, untold spiritual power is being released. God is at work. This is holy ground…take off your shoes. And watch, prayerfully watch, what unfolds.

The other extreme to avoid is minimization. As an alternative offer thanks. Thank your friend for sharing with you. Remind your friend that her words are a signal of the deeper activity of God in her life. Your friend needs to receive forgiveness; to remember the truth; to let her anxious, striving shoulders down; and just receive grace. She may honestly want to kick you under the table for reminding her of God's activity in her life. Her pride may scream, and she may experience pushback. But hopefully, through your response she will be more aware of God's work on her behalf and in her life as she remembers that God's Son hung on a cross to take away the sins of the world; that He paid the penalty so that she could be released from guilt and shame and be restored into relationship with God. And that a way has been made for her to become a different kind of woman. Perhaps her soul will "crack" just a little, and she will feel the movement of grace. When someone brings a confession to you, be sure to remind them, "That is why Jesus had to die. You are forgiven."

Soul friendships emerge out of the fertile soil of knowing and being known. Over seven years ago when my husband and I first sat in a worship service in the church that is now home, I sat in the back of a large auditorium and for over an hour looked at the backs of heads—lots of heads! As I did so I remember I kept thinking, "I do not know anyone, absolutely no one. And…no one knows me." It was a horrible feeling. And, even as an introvert, one of the first things I resolved to do was "know someone."

This is where it must begin. Get out there and make some connections. Work at it. Know and be known. Then make an honest assessment of what "is" in your life right now and an honest request to God for a soul friendship to start or deepen.

At this point, you may either be feeling grateful for the intimate friendship(s) you have sustained over the years and be eager to go deeper, or you may be feeling depressed to discover that this kind of relationship is available but somehow has eluded you.

One of the first natural places to turn in building a soul friendship is prayer. God routinely moves such mountains and is particularly interested in meeting you right at this tender place of openness to relational connection.

Scripture urges us to bring our requests to God frequently, even relentlessly. Pray and then pay close attention to the things that begin to happen around you.

One final note about soul friendships: once you have developed a soul friendship, be sure to pray with your soul friend. When we resolve to know one another and to encourage one another without agendas and without fixing, the most natural response to an authentic sharing of life with a Godward orientation is to hit our knees together. Soul friends pray for each other, even when they are apart. When we talk and pray that engages a whole new level of spiritual power.

12. Simplicity

Simplicity is the spiritual practice of total surrender and abandonment to God. It is having a singularity of heart or purpose.

For many years I lived with a misconception of simplicity. My initial reaction to the word, even when discussed as a spiritual discipline, was to think of streamlining my life by cutting things out and getting rid of material possessions. When it comes to spiritual practices, however, simplicity means to have a singularity of heart and purpose: Jesus—the Main thing, my One thing. And, yes, this can mean having to streamline our lives if necessary in order to make Him the number one priority.

Henry Blackaby in his Bible study, *Experiencing God*, says, "We are a doing people. We feel worthless or useless if we are not busy doing something. Scripture leads us to understand that God is saying, 'I want you to love Me above everything else. When you are in a relationship of love with Me, you have everything there is.' To be loved by God is the highest relationship, the greatest achievement, and the noblest position in life."[23]

Our identity, worth, meaning, and joy are in Christ alone. It is not in our performance, our possessions, our position, or in what people think of us. This is why the Apostle Paul urges us 110 times in his New Testament letters to place ourselves "in Christ."

Christ is to be our singular focus. Time with Him enriches and deepens the relationship we already have with Him.

"This year, let us ask God to dissolve all our hopes (however good they may be!) into a single hope: to know Christ and to be found in Him. May this be a year of desire radically transformed, a deeper, truer, knowing of Christ as our All-Sufficient One."[24]

Nicole Whitacre

Let God know this is a journey you are willing to take and then pursue it whole-heartedly.

As you are pursuing this singularity of heart and of purpose, the most important thing to remember is to make sure that you are living to please God and no one else. Learn to live for an Audience of One.

On the following pages are a few ways to help create or maintain a singularity of heart. Each of these disciplines is often classified as a spiritual practice in and of itself. I include them here as practices that serve to aid in turning our focus toward Christ.

Journaling

Journaling is an invaluable tool for caring for your soul. It can also be used in connection with any of the spiritual practices: prayer, use of Scripture, soul searching, and each of the others. Journaling is the practice of being honest with God in writing about what is currently going on in your life.

For years, the most common picture of journaling was someone sitting down in a quiet place with a blank page and a pen or pencil, pouring out their heart on a page. Today there are many, many nontraditional and creative ways to journal: type your thoughts out in an online diary or illustrate, color, or sketch them.

Begin to consider how you are "wired" by God. Then take a look at some of the creative journaling methods in the Resource Section and give one a try.

Why?

Because the spiritual practice of journaling helps to make your thoughts and prayers more concrete. It helps you to focus on your topic and on speaking to God. And journaling serves as a spiritual record of what has been going on in your life.

As you journal, be honest. It is not always easy, but it is so important to take time to reflect and to think about what is going on in a particular situation.

> *"The Lord is near to all who call on him, to all who call on him in truth."*
> Psalm 145:18

Meditiation

The definition of meditation is continued or extended thought; reflection and contemplation. According to the dictionary definition then, everyone meditates.

The question is, "On what do you meditate?" What do you spend time thinking about? What captures your mind, controls your thoughts, and dominates the desires of your heart?

Focusing our thoughts on the things of God is one way to move toward singularity of heart and of purpose. This does not mean ignoring reality to always look on the bright side of things. Biblical faith never requires us to deny reality in any way. For example, Abraham considered the harsh biological facts of his situation, but he did not weaken in faith (Romans 4:19).

It does mean not allowing the realities of life to dominate our meditation or control our thoughts. We can choose to face realities without allowing them to dominate. Joshua, for example, was facing the most daunting of tasks; however, he was counseled by God to focus on God, not on the task (see Joshua 1:9).

Biblical faith considers the reality of life in a fallen world; yet chooses to make the Lord its meditation. Meditate on the power, wisdom, and love of your Father. By meditating on God you will be reminded that He is interminably greater than any problem you could ever experience.

Observing the Christian Calendar & Traditions

Why celebrate the Christian calendar as a spiritual practice?

Because we live inside a big story. A story that started long before our birth and that will go on long after our earthly death. A story that is as wide as the universe and as old as eternity. The Story of God as centered in Jesus the Christ.

Because we want to inhabit the still-unfolding story of God and have it inhabit and change us. This is exactly what the spiritual practice of living the Christian calendar helps us to do.

Modern day Christ-followers typically celebrate Christmas and Easter, high points in our year, as part of our normal calendar observances; however, most often this does very little to nourish our soul. What if we, as believers, regarded the entire calendar as sacred.

Until just a few years ago, I was totally unaware that the Christian year consisted of more than a few special holy days. When introduced to the Christian calendar, I was amazed to learn that it actually contains whole seasons of spiritual meaning. Perhaps, like me, you are somewhat familiar with the seasons of Advent and Lent or have at least heard of them. But, do you think of Easter as season or know much about the observances called Epiphany and Pentecost?

The Christian year entails, in fact, a sequence of seven seasons built around the holy days that correspond to the major events in the life of Jesus. Observing this calendar is a practice that will help to nourish our soul and move us toward a singularity of heart.

Another practice that helps move us toward singularity of heart is the establishment and observance of traditions.

In the sixth chapter of Deuteronomy, Moses is instructed to write and deliver the message from God that certain values were to be "handed down" to generation after generation.

We term the practice of handing down stories, beliefs, customs, legends, and other such things from one generation to another in order to establish and reinforce a strong sense of identity ("tradition").

Although the word "tradition" is not found in the Old Testament, tradition is there. God established it in Deuteronomy chapter six, the Passover, and the Festival of Booths just to name a few. God IS the inventor of tradition, just as He is the inventor and giver of every good gift.

As we consider incorporating the practice of tradition in our lives, it is important we keep in the forefront of our minds that the tradition is the means, not the end. Traditions are not something to be carried out for their own sake. Their value is in their meaning. Our soul is nourished and our focus is singularized in the meaning.

Many of the traditions established by our Heavenly Father in the Old Testament were done so as a means of helping the people look backward and forward.

Similarly, most of our special days are celebrations of significant events in the past. Birthdays, weddings, anniversaries, holidays, and funerals provide opportunity to look back, and in looking back, remember God's presence and work in our lives.

These same tradition-filled occasions also provide an opportunity for us to look forward. In looking forward to the upcoming celebration, we get a small taste of the emotions to come on the special day itself. And our experience on that special day helps us anticipate the great day when we will encounter our God face to face.

In the looking back, memories. In the looking forward, anticipation. Our memories of past special days help us know what to expect and increase our anticipation of the special days yet to come.

God established special days such as the Passover celebration in the Old Testament. The thought and preparation that went into those very special celebrations and all that surrounded them kept them from passing just like any other day. They provided anchor.

Just as special days were needed in Old Testament times, they are needed today. Special days help us remember who He is and how He works. They rekindle our love for Him and increase our knowledge of Him. They provide anchor for us and for our families.

Practicing the Presence of God

We must keep the Lord God continually before our minds. This is the first and most basic thing we can and must do. David knew this secret and wrote, *"I have set the LORD continually before me; Because He is at my right hand, I will not be shaken. Therefore my heart is glad and my glory rejoices; My flesh also will dwell securely"* (Psalm 16:8–9, NASB).

> *"This is the fundamental secret of caring for our souls. Our part in thus practicing the presence of God is to direct and redirect our minds constantly to Him. In the early time of our "practicing" we may well be challenged by our burdensome habits of dwelling on things less than God. But these are habits—not the law of gravity—and can be broken. A new, grace-filled habit will replace the former ones as we take intentional steps toward keeping God before us. Soon our minds will return to God as the needle of a compass constantly returns to the north. If God is the great longing of our souls, He will become the pole star of our inward beings."*[25] Dallas Willard

As a beginning step in this "practicing" process, we can choose to practice constantly returning our minds to God in Christ. There are several ways to return your mind to God. Try preaching or talking to yourself (see "Learn to Talk to Yourself" in this section), or you can sing worship choruses, hymns, or Scripture. Whatever you choose to preach, say, or sing; make sure it is good theology.

Today we often feel we must "get away" from our daily routine in order to worship God, but that is only because we have not learned to practice His presence at all times. Lay brother, Brother Lawrence (*The Practice of the Presence of God*) found it easy to worship God through the common tasks of life. He did not have to go away for special spiritual retreats.

Learn to practice the presence of God in your daily life by memorizing great passages from Scripture. Passages such as Matthew 7, John 14–17, 1 Corinthians 13, and Colossians 3 are wonderful "soul nourishing" selections. The practice of memorizing Scripture is essential to our soul's health and a key to practicing the presence of God, for as we fill our minds with passages of His word and have them available for our meditation, "quiet time" takes over the entirety of our lives.

Practicing the presence of God is not only about memorizing Scripture. That is just one aspect. Practicing the presence of God is about paying attention, and "paying attention" is difficult in our culture of busyness and noise. Many of us, in fact, have allowed ourselves to get caught up in a way of life that does not set us up to pay attention to the presence of God. We must recognize this and intentionally set about to become noticers—abandoning ourselves to the presence of God and His work in our lives. We must learn to live with an ongoing awareness of the living, active, Holy God who has chosen to spend His days with us.

> "We must know before we can love.
> In order to know God, we must often think of Him;
> and when we come to love Him, we shall then also think of Him often,
> for our heart will be with our treasure."[26]
> Brother Lawrence

How can we set ourselves up to be more aware?

- Set an alarm on our phone that says, "Remember Jesus."

- Place silly little stickers or post-it notes that cause us to pause and think on God's presence right then and there on the dash of our car, on our phone, beside our bed, or anywhere.

- Practice My One Word (see the Resources Section) for a year and select a word that by its very definition would lead you to notice God's presence in your life. Try a word like "see." Then look for God in every conversation, connection, and circumstance. This practice will help you learn that God is easy to find and that enjoying Him in the everyday moments of life is extraordinary. When you see God, really see Him at work in the details, it will also help you to know His sovereign hand and presence. This is a natural relief from worry, achievement, and self-reliance.

- Acknowledge Him moment by moment. Speak out loud to Him. Be aware that He is with you. You might even pretend to be on the phone as you converse with Him. There is just something about speaking out loud that builds faith in His presence.

- Identify a "trigger." A trigger is something that when you see it, you are immediately reminded of God's love—God IS love, God loves me, God is loving me right now! The best triggers have life: birds, water, children. Be constantly reminded of His love and maybe even reply with an audible, "I love you, too, Lord."

Sabbath

While we saw in practicing the presence of God that it is not necessary to "get away" in order to practice His presence, some time away is good for us (Solitude and Silence).

God instituted the Sabbath and it is one of His most beautiful gifts to us. It is a delightful treat that He has not kept to Himself but shares freely with us. *"Remember the Sabbath day, to keep it holy"* (Exodus 20:8).

Through the Sabbath, God asks us to slow down so we once again become awestruck by His goodness in our lives, our relationships, and the world. The Sabbath provides the opportunity to nurture our appreciation for the beauty of creation, the deliciousness of provision, and the joy of celebration.

But observing the Sabbath, like so many of the spiritual practices that we need for soul nourishment, is difficult for most of us. While Jesus calls, *"Come to me, all who labor and are heavy laden, and I will give you rest. Take my yoke upon you, and learn from me, for I am gentle and lowly in heart, and you will find rest for your souls. For my yoke is easy, and my burden is light"* (Matthew 11:28–30), we find we have yoked ourselves to many things other than Christ. We have yoked ourselves to the expectations of others (or what we "think" those expectations are), commitments that were not ours to make, busyness, activity, unhealthy relationships, projects, and so many other "things" that keep us from the rest our God designed for us.

Have you ever noticed that immediately after Jesus' invitation to "take [His] yoke… and find rest," He taught on the Sabbath (Matthew 12)? The Sabbath is a device for unyoking. It is a gift in time and space that has been set apart for us to occupy with God. A gift that gives us pause to de-yoke from all of the unhealthy tethers in our lives.

In order to observe the Sabbath, we must become deliberate and intentional. We must put it on our calendars, make preparation, and follow through. In our beginning efforts we will probably also need to incorporate solitude with Jesus as we practice this spiritual discipline.

To keep a Sabbath is to set aside a twenty-four-hour day in which you do no work in order to rest in God's person and provision. Sabbath is a time to refrain from your normal responsibilities in order to pray and play with God and others. A Sabbath is NOT the same thing as a day off. A Sabbath day is dedicated to the Lord. Even as you relax or enjoy being with friends and family you maintain a prayerful focus. The New Testament teaches that any day of the week can be set aside as a Sabbath day (Romans 14:3–6).

Start where you are. Begin now to master the art of ceasing, because it is in the ceasing that we truly rest. Make time to pause, to rest. It is a command from our Father. Apart from this time, we cannot ever fully awaken to the presence of God with us.

So then, there remains a Sabbath rest for the people of God, for whoever has entered God's rest has also rested from his works as God did from his. Let us therefore strive to enter that rest, so that no one may fall by the same sort of disobedience.

Hebrews 4:9-11

Spiritual Markers

And the people of Israel did just as Joshua commanded and took up twelve stones out of the midst of the Jordan, according to the number of the tribes of the people of Israel, just as the Lord told Joshua. And they carried them over with them to the place where they lodged and laid them down there.

Joshua 4:8

Spiritual memory is crucial in the Christian life. Do you vividly recall times when you know God spoke to you? It would be tragic if, in your haste to advance in your Christian faith, you neglected to leave spiritual markers at the key crossroads of your life. Without the help of these markers, you will lose your spiritual bearings. The Israelites experienced a tumultuous pilgrimage. Their doubt that God was powerful enough to give them victory cost them forty years of wandering in the wilderness. Then God miraculously parted the waters of the Jordan River so they could pass over and continue their conquest. God knew that at times the Israelites would face intimidating enemies and would need a reminder that He was powerful enough to protect them.

The Israelites might be tempted to think they made a mistake entering Canaan. For this reason, God instructed them to build a monument on the banks of the Jordan River. Whenever they returned to this spot, they would see the monument and be reminded of God's awesome power and His mighty act on their behalf. This marker would give them confidence to meet the new challenges they faced. The marker also provided the people with opportunities to teach their children about God's activity on behalf of His people.

A spiritual marker identifies a time of decision, direction, or transition when you clearly knew that God guided you. Can you remember the moment you became a child of God? Were there specific times when He called you to His ways of living? Can you point to times when He clearly guided you in a decision? Were there times when He spoke powerfully to you about a commitment you should make? Keep track of these important moments! Regularly rehearse them and notice the steady progression in the way God has led you. Use your spiritual markers as the Israelites did—to be reminded of God's awesome power and His mighty acts on your behalf and as opportunities to teach your children and grandchildren about God's activity within your family.

If identifying your spiritual markers is new to you, here are a couple of ideas to get you thinking:

List/Journal
Simply make a list on a sheet of paper or in your spiritual journal. Pull away to a quiet place for a bit and think on your life. Write down those moments when you knew God was guiding you. Then over the next hours or even days as other "moments" come to mind, add them to your list.

Timeline
Again, with paper and pen or pencil, sit quietly with the Lord. Devote this time to thinking back over your life and to creating a timeline of the major events. From this timeline, you will be able to identify many personal spiritual markers.

Stones
Just as the Israelites did in Joshua 4:8, gather some stones of remembrance. Go outside and pick up some stones. Then as you sit with the Lord, think back and identify the spiritual markers of your life. Write each on a stone.

Jewelry
In identifying the spiritual markers in my own life I began with a list; however, I did not want to leave it as a list. My desire was to find a way to "set up a monument" that I would pass by often. For my monument, I chose a bracelet because I had also been looking for a piece of jewelry that I could wear as a symbol or reminder of who I belong to. My choice was to combine the two. I purchased a bracelet of the European charm variety and then began searching for just the right bead to represent each of my spiritual markers. This bracelet is now one of my most valued possessions. I wear it almost daily, and each time I glance at it I am reminded of God's "life-from-the-dead" power on my behalf, of who He is, and of who I am in Him. An added bonus to this type of monument: my grandchildren are drawn to my bracelet. The beads on the bracelet have created and continue to create

such wonderful opportunities for me to share my Savior and His work in my life and in the lives of our family with my grandchildren!

Are you ready to identify your own personal spiritual markers? Schedule a date, pull away from your routine, and begin by making a list or a timeline of your own. Then begin rehearsing them, over and over, in order to be reminded of God's awesome power and work in your life.

This is an absolutely amazing practice for drawing your heart toward Him and moving you toward singularity of purpose.

Submission

The spiritual practice of submission is about not asserting ourselves in order to come under the authority, wisdom, and power of Jesus Christ as our Lord, King, and Master. It is about denying ourselves the power or privilege we want.

> *Humble yourselves, therefore, under the mighty hand of God*
> *so that at the proper time he may exalt you.*
> 1 Peter 5:6

Jesus says to us, "Trust Me. Put aside your striving, your control, your manipulating and simply trust Me."

In practicing submission, we are choosing not to make things happen for ourselves and not to control people or situations, even if we can. We are choosing instead to come under the Lord's authority, wisdom, and power. We are choosing to trust His sovereignty.

I love this phrase from Dallas Willard, "Abandon outcomes to God" (in *Renovation of the Heart*, 318). Adopting this phrase as a personal mantra might help as one is learning to live a life of submission to God.

Another phrase I picked up from a dear mentor a few years ago is, "Jesus, You are Lord of _____ (fill in the blank with whatever it is that you are struggling to turn over to God—my job, my children, my home, whether this task will get done today, whether someone will step up to take on this responsibility, etc). I entered a personal relationship with Jesus as a young child and grew up in the church. I knew the words, "Jesus is Lord of all." It made a huge difference in my life, however, when I was able to release things one-by-one to His Lordship, and it certainly helped to draw my heart and purpose toward Him.

Surrender

The spiritual practice of Surrender is very closely related to that of submission. Surrender is simple trust. Can I, will I trust God, no matter what He chooses for my day?

The heart of man plans his way, but the LORD establishes his steps.

Proverbs 16:9

Surrender can also be a struggle. It can be hard to turn the details of our lives over to God—to trust Him, no matter what. Following are three ways that may help in learning to surrender.

Daily Status Meetings with God

This is NOT a devotional time. It is a business meeting—at a desk with your planner/calendar open. Your daily status meeting with God is a time to prayerfully review your daily calendar. As you do, ask His guidance for the appointments and tasks that are scheduled for your week. Focus on plans you have made, rather than obligations others have suggested for you. This is a time for refocusing on your goals and priorities. It is also the time to surrender everything—your plans, your priorities, your goals—back to God.

Many are the plans in the mind of a man,
but it is the purpose of the LORD that will stand.

Proverbs 19:21

As you review your plans and align your soul during your daily status meeting, try to listen to Him as you pray, "Show me your purpose, Lord."

Daily status meetings with God are necessary in order to navigate the "overwhelms." And who is there among us that does not daily navigate the "overwhelms?"

God has given us a purpose to fulfill while we are here on this earth. We need this daily status meeting with our Purpose-Giver to ensure that we are aligning our daily commitments to His purposes and to receive direction from Him as to how we are to fulfill that purpose.

Grace Breaks

The observance of grace breaks will provide a much-needed respite during your day. Grace breaks are a brief time set aside for the purpose of reviewing things that God spoke to you during your morning quiet time together.

So often we enjoy such a sweet time of communion with our Heavenly Father during our morning quiet time, even at times to the point of being overcome by something He has revealed to us. Then, we are off—so much to do, so many places to be, people demanding our time and energy—never giving it another thought.

We need time. Time to recall. Time to remember.

Begin the practice of taking grace breaks. Set an alarm on your phone, set the kitchen timer, or associate your grace break time with something you are already doing such as preparing or eating meals. When the alarm goes off, when it is time to eat, take a few minutes to recall, remember, and reflect upon what God is speaking to you.

"Dollarama Canvas"

This idea comes from a blog post by Kathy Butryn and I love it. As soon as I read the post, I ran to my nearest dollar store to purchase a wee little canvas and easel for myself. (I was unable to find one there but did locate one at a favorite craft store!)

In her post, Kathy suggested that we purchase a small canvas and easel as an aid in surrendering our day to the Lord. Once purchased, place the easeled canvas in a spot that is seen often and leave the canvas blank.

The little blank canvas represents our day. It serves as a daily reminder that even though we tend to pre-paint the canvas of our day by planning our daily activities, God is the One who ultimately determines the course of our day.

When you look at your little blank canvas be reminded that He will paint your day. And ask yourself if you are willing to accept all of His assignments for the day. Will you surrender to His will for your day, no matter what?

Learn to Talk to Yourself

Consider the following:

You are running late for work one morning and still need to drop the children at school. You are rushing, trying to herd everyone toward the car when suddenly everything halts at the sound of a loud crash of glass breaking. You spin back toward the source of the sound to see your five-year-old, standing frozen, tears flowing. Your gaze then lands on an almost whole gallon of milk quickly covering the kitchen floor and a shattered casserole dish nearby. In that moment, staring at the scene before you, you lose it as your inner dialogue revs up. "Why me? Why now? What was he trying to do? Don't they all know I do not have time for this? It is going to take me forever to clean this up. I'm going to be late. The kids will be late. Why does this stuff ALWAYS happen to me? Where is (name of spouse) when I need him?" And on and on it goes.

Do you realize that you are constantly talking to yourself? Constantly. All the time. Differing research indicates that our inner dialog consists of somewhere between 150–1,300 words a minute. Yes, that is a huge range, but either way it results in a lot of dialogue. Do the calculations, and we discover that we are speaking to our own soul between 47,000 and 51,000 sentences a day!

Frankly, most of our inner dialogue is very neutral. "Oh, I am really not ready to crawl out of bed just yet." "Where did I put my keys?" "I can't forget to pick the kids up from piano at four." "What am I going to fix for dinner?" There is a portion of our inner dialogue, however, that is NOT neutral. It is, in fact, destructive—meaning that the dialogue is not at all soul nourishing.

It is this destructive inner dialogue that is so harmful to us. It is not truth, and in listening to it we are actually speaking lies to our own soul.

Allow me to suggest that rather than listening to ourselves, to the inner dialogue that is so adept at throwing "me-focused pity parties," we begin to practice talking to ourselves. Let's go back to the scenario at the beginning of this section.

What if, instead of listening to the entire inner dialogue play out after the crash of glass, the following were to occur:

Two or three "whys or whats" into your inner dialogue, you stop, take a breath, and instead of continuing to listen, you begin to talk to yourself with purpose and intent. "You are right, Lord. This is not about me. Everything is about you. Forgive me for my self-focus. Thank you that no one was hurt. Thank you for this precious little image-bearer that you have entrusted to my care. Thank you that he has a heart to help. Thank you, Lord, for dying for me and for my sin of self-centeredness. Take my self-centeredness now. I give it to you. Please, help my children to see You through me right now."

This is not our natural inclination. It is not easy. We cannot do it on our own. We must ask for God's help in learning to surrender everything, even our inner dialogue. Invite the Holy Spirit in and ask Him to nudge you when your inner dialogue becomes destructive. Plead for the opening of your spiritual eyes and ears that you would become aware of the Holy Spirit's presence and work in your life. Pray that you would be conscious of the dialogue taking place in your inner self.

The Bible tells us that the life we are living right now is a direct reflection of our thoughts, or our inner dialogue. Proverbs 23:7 says, *As [s]he thinks in [her] heart, so is [s]he* (NKJV).

Today is the best time to begin the spiritual practice of talking to yourself. Be aware. When you hear the destructive inner dialogue begin, stop! DO NOT LISTEN. Take a breath and begin talking to yourself. Share statements of truth. Preach the gospel. The gospel (truth) is always constructive. Truth builds up. It brings life. And it leads to singularity of heart and purpose.

> *We destroy arguments and every lofty opinion raised against the knowledge of God, and take every thought captive to obey Christ.*
>
> 2 Corinthians 10:5

Thanksgiving

The dictionary definition of thanksgiving is "grateful acknowledgment of benefits or favors, especially to God; an expression of thanks, especially to God."[27]

For the believer in Christ, thanksgiving should be a perpetual and ongoing expression, as natural as breathing—paying tribute to God the Father by paying attention; seeing the glory, naming the graces.

It has been said that "our human experience is the sum of what our soul sees. And our soul sees precisely what we attend to." What a convincing argument for the significance of soul nourishment. For if we neglect our soul, what is our human experience?

Purpose to nourish your soul. Help your soul to see, for it is only through paying attention and offering grateful acknowledgement that we learn to see. See the glory; name the graces, not as an end, but as a means—a means of gazing into the heart of God.

See Him here. See Him now. This is where God is. He is here in the present. His very name claims it—I AM.

As you begin to practice the discipline of thanksgiving, be mindful that it is easy to learn to notice, to count gifts, and to give thanks when our circumstances are good. But what about when things are hard, and sometimes they are very hard? In those difficult times it is essential that as we pay attention we remember our focus is God. With our focus rightly on God, we can come to the place of being able to express gratitude in the midst of every situation. Thankfulness is the acknowledgement that God can redeem every situation and make us more than triumphant in any circumstance (see Romans 8:13–19).

This is the beauty of thankfulness. A grateful heart invites us to a shift in our relationship with God and with others. In it we are invited to journey from loss to trust, from pain to praise, from multiplicity to singularity.

Yes, you! You are His divine choice! What does that do for your heart? Isn't it time to live in this knowledge, all the time? He chose you, and He chose you to live fully! Live with astonished gratitude. Live in awed wonder. Live in overwhelming joy. Live utterly free. Fully live the fullest life!

Worship

Worship is the spiritual practice of praising God's greatness, goodness, and beauty in words, music, ritual, and/or silence.

The Merriam-Webster Dictionary defines worship as: (1) To honor or reverence as a divine being or supernatural power; (2) To regard with great or extravagant respect, honor, or devotion; (3) To perform or take part in worship or an act of worship.

Worship to our Heavenly Father can be offered anytime, anywhere, and in a multitude of ways. Yes, it is singing. Yes, worship can be many believers gathered in a church lifting their voices together before a sermon. But it is so much more—it is an opportunity to adore and to honor God! Worship can be the extending of grace to a child, deferring to your spouse in a disputed matter, enjoying a sunset, or washing the dishes.

The wise Puritan, Thomas Watson, wrote:

> The first fruit of love is the musing of the mind upon God. He who is in love, his thoughts are ever upon the object. He who loves God is ravished and transported with the contemplation of God. "When I awake, I am still with thee" (Ps. 139:18). The thoughts are as travelers in the mind. David's thoughts kept heav-

> en-road. "I am still with Thee." God is the treasure, and where the treasure is, there is the heart. By this we may test our love to God. What are our thoughts most upon? Can we say we are ravished with delight when we think on God? Have our thoughts got wings? Are they fled aloft? Do we contemplate Christ and glory? ... A sinner crowds God out of his thoughts. He never thinks of God, unless with horror, as the prisoner thinks of the judge.[28]

What are your thoughts most focused on? Can you say you are ravished with delight when you think of God? When you think of God does it cause you to praise His greatness, goodness, and beauty?

Worship should become the constant undertone of our lives. It is the single most powerful force in completing and sustaining restoration of our whole being to God.

Worship is the primary nourishment for our soul. Refresh your soul through praise and worship. Then experience the power of the indwelling Christ flowing from you to others as you walk constantly with God. By stepping with Him in the flow of His grace, we live with spontaneity, love our neighbors, and minister the word and power of the gospel.

Worship is both the language and the key. It is the language of victorious spiritual experience. It is the key to unlocking the door to great treasures of grace. Worship is central to the life of God in the soul. Worship will turn you toward making Christ your One thing.

> *"Worship is the believer's response of all that they are—mind, emotions, will, body—to what God is and says and does."*[29]
>
> Warren Wiersbe

YES or NO

I must admit that this is one spiritual discipline that I have had extreme difficulty with over the years—as a young mom, working mom, mom of teens, and even as an empty nester. This one has plagued me!

This spiritual practice has also been referred to as planned neglect—intentionally neglecting the things that countless people want us to do, so we will be available to do what God wants. It is the deliberate act of weighing what we can or should say *yes* to against what we need to say *no* to.

Many of us have a propensity to say *yes* to good things. So, the first thing we need to learn is that "good" does not require a yes! There are a multitude of good things to be done; even great things. Our first priority is not in saying yes it is in making sure we are listening. To God. To do this, we must put our ear to His word, pray, and seek His face. We need, first, to be available, listening to God and then following Him when He brings those totally unexpected divine appointments to us.

If we are booked so solid there is no room in our schedules for unanticipated God moments, we will miss them. We must learn to say no to people concerning the vast majority of very good things they invite us to, in order to be available to say yes to God concerning the small number of things He truly calls us to. Overbooking our lives can cause us to miss out on some of life's greatest joys, opportunities, and occasions for gratitude.

Whether you call it yes or no or planned neglect, the act must be intentional. Saying no (planned neglect) makes room for God. If you do not give yourself room to breathe, you will not give God room to move.

> *"But one thing is necessary. Mary has chosen the good portion, which will not be taken away from her."*
> Luke 10:42

As you begin to think about creating room for God to move in your life, remember that rather than having a large number of causes you have little investments in, it is better to have a much smaller number that you are wholeheartedly engaged in. In this way, you will be able to give your very best.

Not sure what to remove from your already overly-crowded plate or where to say no? Ask God for wisdom as to which these should be, and He will give it (see James 1:5).

From here on out, when presented with a new opportunity, practice invoking the spiritual practice of yes or no. God grants permission for you to say NO to anything that will keep you from being able to say yes to His best for you. You might even want to adopt a new mantra:

"Unless it's a definite YES, it's a NO"...

or a new philosophy:

"I will NEVER say YES without asking God whether this is one of those exceptional things He really wants me to do. I will tell Him that unless He smacks me in the side of the head and makes it clear, I will assume He DOES NOT want me to do it."

Learn to weigh your YES and NO responses in order that you do not veer away from Christ. Make Jesus your singular focus.

> *Therefore, since we are surrounded by so great a cloud of witnesses, let us also lay aside every weight, and sin which clings so closely, and let us run with endurance the race that is set before us, looking to Jesus, the founder and perfecter of our faith, who for the joy that was set before him endured the cross, despising the shame, and is seated at the right hand of the throne of God (Hebrews 12:1–2).*

> *"But seek first the kingdom of God and his righteousness, and all these things will be added to you"* (Matthew 6:33).

PART 3
Resources
FOR NOURISHING THE SOUL

INTRODUCTION TO
Resources

For God alone, O my soul, wait in silence, for my hope is from him.

Psalm 62:5

Life is busy. Life is hard.

We so often have every good intention of spending alone time with God, but it rarely seems to happen. Sometimes it is an issue of over-crowded schedules. Sometimes it is a matter of mixed-up priorities. Sometimes it is simply that we do not have any idea how to "do" alone time or where to begin.

Perhaps this is you. You hear the longing cries of your soul—cries for intimacy with God. You want to nourish your soul. You just never seem to be able to find the time. You have no idea "how" or where to begin. You are "hungry."

The resources in the section have been compiled for you.

Blessed child of the Living God, I have been where you are now—taking care of my home; caring for toddlers, school-aged children, teens; working outside my home; going back to college full-time as a nontraditional student; ministering at church—in other words, trying to balance a very full plate. A plate I piled high, with good things even, but one that left me little time to be alone with God, much less to figure out what this time should look like.

These resources are for you. Take them…and use them to feed your soul.

Most of the included resources are ready to use. Peruse the collection. Look for ones that call out to you. Notice which of the spiritual disciplines is being targeted and how so many of them overlap. Which one will you choose to feed on first? Then take the first bite. Nourish that longing soul deep within you.

Be intentional. Carve out the time. And then persevere—continuing on, never giving up.

And as you live a life of soul nourishment, take encouragement by evaluating your progress from time to time with these two questions:

1. Do I love God more today than I did before?

2. How well do I obey His Word?

God's blessings to you as you begin the fruitful work of nourishing your soul.

If we live by the Spirit, let us also keep in step with the Spirit.
Galatians 5:25

General

SOUL NOURISHMENT RESOURCES

1. A Check-up for Your Soul

1. Create a list of words to describe your soul as it is right now. Use the following words to get started. Include any other words that come to mind.

   - peace
   - self-absorption
   - shame
   - giving and receiving grace
   - apathy
   - generosity of spirit
   - joy
   - ability to trust
   - physical fatigue
   - discernment
   - isolation
   - toxic anger
   - compassion
   - humility
   - feelings of depression
   - creativity
   - panic
   - insecurity
   - callousness
   - stronger temptation to sin
   - a judgmental attitude
   - vision
   - cynicism
   - balance and focus
   - lack of desire for God
   - love

2. Now, divide your list into two columns: Neglect & Health. Place positive words in the Health column and negative words in the Neglect column.

3. How does your list look? Is your soul healthy, or is it showing major signs of neglect?

4. Take some time to reflect on your list.

   > How do you feel about your assessment? Are you resisting what appears on your list? Does it feel false? Hopeless? Desirable?

   > Write out your results.

You can spend your time and energy in an attempt to decrease the symptoms of soul neglect and increase the symptoms of soul health, however, when we focus on the symptoms rather than the cause our results are short-lived and possibly counterproductive. Why not focus on the source of the trauma, a neglected soul?

5. Spend some time in prayer over your list and your written response to it. Ask God to reveal your areas of greatest need and to help you nourish your soul back to health.

A soul is healthy to the extent that it maintains a strong connection and receptivity to God.[30]

2. Creating a Personal Sacred Space

God can meet us anywhere and everywhere. Yet, there are those places, those times, and those people in our lives through whom we tend to experience God's presence more readily. It is NOT that God is more available, but rather that we are more open and aware.

Creating a Sacred Space is the INTENTIONAL act of making space for God.

ASK:
> What will help me draw closer to God?
> What will act as a distraction from God?

The answers to these questions will help guide you into choosing what should and should not be part of your Sacred Space.

Ideas of Items for a Sacred Space:

- comfy chair (with an ottoman)
- Bible
- lamp
- journal
- small table
- sketch pad
- tablecloth or doily
- pen/pencils
- small cross
- colored pencils/markers
- smooth stone
- rug
- candle
- floor pillows
- incense or fragrance
- music
- wall art/photographs

According to Charissa at Grace Works studio, "[Your Sacred Space] should be tailor-made just for you—a place where you are comfortable, that resonates with who you are, and helps you to focus on and connect with God. Your Sacred Space can be anywhere; however, it can reflect through music and art a location where you especially connect with God. Take some time to think about the times and places in your life where you have felt close to God. Use this as the framework for creating your Sacred Space. Also, be sure to include in this space the tools you regularly use when connecting with God."[31]

You will grow in your spiritual walk. As you do, your Sacred Space should change to reflect your growth.

REMEMBER: A Sacred Space is merely a tool just like our journals and verse maps. The purpose of this tool is to provide a place where we can regularly go and connect with God and self.

3. Ways to Draw Closer to God

Through Prayer

1. Pray. Commit your day to God before your feet hit the floor in the morning.
2. Have a daily appointment with God. Pray about your appointments and your to-do list.
3. Once a week or whenever possible, pray with your soul friend.
4. Take a "prayer walk." Pray for your neighbors, schools, churches, and businesses as you pass by.
5. Pray Scripture.
6. Pray in color.
7. Thank God every time you appreciate His creation (sunsets, rainbows, waterfalls, etc.).
8. Breathe 'breath' prayers.
9. Engage your body when you pray: dance, pace, stretch, or choose different postures.
10. Join in corporate prayer.
11. Set the timer on your phone as a reminder to stop and pray.
12. Pray as you walk, run, ride your bike, or walk the dog.
13. Say His name—"Jesus." Out loud.
14. When you are unable to turn off your brain, thank God for the people and things ping-ponging around in your head, even in the middle of the night.
15. Crochet, brush you hair, or do the laundry as you pray.
16. Pray through the alphabet for your family, your schedule, your elected officials, etc.
17. Write down your prayers.
18. Have a heart-to-heart with God. Share your deepest concerns, fears, and thanks with Him.
19. Adopt a missionary to pray for and to support.

Through Time in Scripture

20. Study and meditate on the attributes of God.

21. Study and meditate on the names of Jesus.

22. Study and meditate on the roles of the Holy Spirit.

23. Do a study on God's love for you.

24. Read the Bible daily.

25. Read God's Word privately and publicly.

26. Read Scripture for pleasure.

27. Read God's Word with a pen in hand.

28. Read biographies of the saints.

29. Read the Bible in a different translation.

30. Put yourself in the Bible account you are reading. Observe. Ask questions.

31. Write out Scripture—by hand.

32. Set aside time to meditate on the Word of God.

33. Paint as you reflect or meditate upon a Scripture passage.

34. Memorize key verses and passages.

35. Try *Lectio Divina*.

36. Personalize Bible promises.

37. Choose a life verse.

38. Verse Map a favorite Bible verse or one from a current study.

39. Select a Bible verse as the screen saver on your computer.

40. Decorate your home with Scripture art.

41. Use a Bible verse-a-day calendar.

42. Keep a devotional book in the bathroom.

43. Teach a Bible study or Sunday school class.

44. Teach your children a memory verse each week.

45. Join a weekly Bible study.

46. Write a key verse on the top of each day's to-do list.

47. Make a list of what you learned about God every time you read the Bible.

48. Try your hand at Illustrated Bible Journaling (search it on Google).

49. Keep a pencil and paper handy during your quiet time to keep your brain engaged and to remember what you are learning.

Through Solitude and Silence

50. Spend a day alone with God. Be sure this time is spent away from home. (If a whole day isn't possible, try half of a day.)

51. Set a timer and sit quietly alone with God for five minutes.

52. Go out for the evening with only Jesus as your date.

53. Establish a "Drink Deeply" time. (This is a time set aside simply for enjoying God and not feeling rushed by the next appointment on your list.)

54. Set aside a special place to meet with God that doesn't overlook any mess or unfinished work.

55. Place an empty chair across from you or at your table. Image Jesus sitting in that chair as you talk with Him.

Through Soul Searching

56. Pay attention to your "stuff."

57. Schedule a dedicated and consistent time for a period of self-reflection.

58. Be honest with God and with yourself.

59. Use a list of great questions as a guide for your soul searching.

60. Keep a journal of your self-reflections.

61. Take a spiritual gifts assessment.

Through Soul Friendships

62. Surround yourself with godly friends.

63. Have a conversation with a soul friend about what the Lord is doing in your life.

64. Ask a godly woman to be your mentor for this particular season of your life.

65. Invite feedback from other Christians.

66. Cultivate a new friendship.

67. Invite friends over for dinner and prayer.

68. Share your dream with someone else.

Through Simplicity

69. Take notes in church and review them daily.

70. Begin a journal.

71. If you are already a journaler, shake things up by trying a new form of journaling. Get creative.

72. Write a life purpose statement.

73. Grab a journal and record 1,000 gifts from God.

74. Write out your God story. Keep it to three minutes in length.

75. Think back over your life and create a list of your Spiritual Markers.

76. Practice a cross-centered day (preach the gospel to yourself, read Scriptures about the cross, listen to music with the message of the cross, etc.).

77. Keep your to-do list beside you. If something comes up during your quiet time, write it down so that you can let it go.

78. Unplug the phone and turn off email during your devotions.

79. Rearrange your priorities so they reflect God's priorities.

80. Learn to say, "No."

81. Take a nap.

82. Take a bubble bath or hot shower.

GENERAL Soul Nourishment Resources

83. Turn off the TV.

84. From time to time, head out to your favorite coffee shop for your devotions.

85. Get plenty of rest at night.

86. Go to church at least once a week.

87. Attend a Christian conference or seminar.

88. Volunteer for a Christian charity.

89. Go for a praise walk thanking God for everything you see.

90. Serve someone more needy than yourself.

91. Donate money to those in need.

92. Visit someone who is ill.

93. Set the timer on your watch to go off every hour to remind you to think of Him.

94. Observe "grace breaks."

95. Consider your God-wiring when choosing ways to draw closer.

96. Sit in a place that is calming and nourishing for you. Change your usual venue.

97. Sing praise songs, hymns, and choruses.

98. Sing Scripture songs with your children as you put them to bed.

99. Sing out loud. Belt it out.

100. Join the choir or praise team.

101. Play worship music or a sermon podcast while you work out, do household chores, or drive your car.

102. Listen to Christian radio.

103. Play your musical instrument as an act of worship.

104. Write a letter to God.

105. Write a poem about God.

106. Give up a favorite food for a month to remind yourself of His worth.

107. Fast.

108. Eat Temple food. Choose not to eat junk food for a day.

109. Stay alert to God's surprises throughout each and every day.

110. Forgive those who have wronged you.

111. Make a list or scrapbook of the things God has done for you.

112. Go through the alphabet naming an attribute of God for each letter.

113. Preach God's Word to your soul.

114. Choose to make duty a delight.

115. Step out in faith in an area that God has placed on your heart.

116. Humble yourself before others.

117. Practice His presence.

118. Keep your eyes open to God's guiding hand in your life.

119. Be honest with God.

120. Wear a special piece of jewelry that will remind you of Jesus.

121. Choose to be content.

122. Confess your sin.

123. Forgive yourself.

124. Do something sacrificial and don't tell anyone about it.

125. Don't listen to gossip.

126. Praise others daily.

127. Obey immediately.

128. Offer a "blessing."

129. Adopt a word for the year.

130. Set goals and plans for greater intimacy with Jesus.

4. Nourish Your Soul A-Z

A. **Ask** God. He is there. All the time. Pursuing. Ask!

B. **Breathe** breath prayers.

C. **Create.**

D. **Develop** soul friendships.

E. **Engage.** Be present. Pay attention.

F. **Fast**, because fasting is feasting.

G. **Grace breaks**. They are good for the soul. Observe a few throughout the day.

H. **Heap praise** and adoration on the Lord.

I. **Invite feedback** from your soul friends. They are FOR you.

J. **Journal.** Write for your soul.

K. **Keep a daily appointment** with the Lord.

L. **Learn to listen.**

M. **Music** speaks to the soul. Listen, sing, dance.

N. **No**—It's okay to say it. Sometimes it's best.

O. **Offer Thanksgiving.** Every day.

P. **Pray** the Bible, **preach** the Gospel to yourself, and **practice** the presence of God.

Q. **Quietly meditate on Scripture** for it is health and life to the soul. *For it is not an idle word for you; indeed it is your life* (Deuteronomy 32:47, NASB).

R. **Read the Bible** with purpose.

S. **Sit at Jesus' feet.**

T. **Talk to yourself.** Learn to spend more time talking to yourself than listening to yourself.

U. **Uncover** your soul's path to God.

V. **Verses.** Identify and claim soul verses.

W. **Wait.** Wait on the Lord. Wait in silence and solitude—with no agenda.

X. **eXamine** your life. Engage in times of self-reflection.

Y. **Yield.** Make Jesus, who IS the one thing, THE one thing. Have a singular purpose.

Z. **Zig and zag** as you take walks, L–O–N–G walks.

5. Ideas for Spending Time with God

- Make a list. What are the things that energize you and make you smile? Take care not to put limits on your list. Be sure to include people, places, interests, things, activities, music, and anything else that comes to mind. Now use your list as a guide for making sure some of these things get put on your weekly calendar.

- Take a walk outside. Before you go, read the first chapter of one of Paul's letters and write down a verse or two you want to meditate on while you walk.

- Contemplate one of the shorter New Testament books. Begin by reading straight through the book a couple of times in order to get the big picture. Read the book again. This time read slower and more deliberately. Focus on a chapter or even less at each reading. As you read, ask yourself these questions: What are the major themes of the book? Which verses stand out to me? How do these themes and verses relate to my life? What action does God want me to take because of this? What does this passage reveal about God?

- Sing a classic hymn and concentrate on the words. Let the message of the Gospel nourish your soul and draw you into God's presence. (Some wonderful old hymns of the faith are "Amazing Grace," "Be Thou My Vision," "Come, Thou Fount," or "It Is Well with My Soul").

- Search your soul. Read the parable of the four soils (Matthew 13:3–23). What does the evidence of your life indicate? As you reflect, ask God to show you which soil you are currently.

- Stand and sing your favorite worship song at the top of your lungs. Raise your hands in worship. Move your feet.

- Journal what is in your heart. Be honest as you write. The following are some ideas to get you started:

    › Father, what I need most right now is…

    › Jesus, my heart is full of…

    › Spirit, heal my… (fear, regret, anger, etc.)

- Simply rest. Recharge your body and spirit. Read Jesus' invitation to rest: *Come to me, all who labor and are heavy laden, and I will give you rest. Take my yoke upon you, and learn from me, for I am gentle and lowly in heart, and you will find rest for your souls. For my yoke is easy, and my burden is light* (Matthew 11:28–30).

- Write out your prayers. Simply pour out your heart onto the paper. Present your most honest fears, hurts, and requests to God. Praise Him that He hears and understands.

- Try the Palm Up, Palm Down Centering Prayer. Sit comfortably and start by placing your hands palm down on your legs. Release all your worries, doubts, and anxieties to God. Then turn your hands palm up and receive God's love and blessing. Remember the words of Psalm 31:19: *Oh, how abundant is your goodness, which you have stored up for those who fear you.*

- Pray the words of Scripture. Try Psalms 16, 25, or 42. Put the Psalm or Scripture into your own words. Insert your own name into the Scripture. Pray from a posture different than the one you usually assume.

- Look at your schedule for the coming week. Pray over every upcoming appointment, project, and social obligation. What do you hear God saying to you about these events? Write it down. For example, does an obligation need to be eliminated because it's from an earlier season in your life? Does the Holy Spirit bring someone to mind as you pray about one of the appointments on your calendar?

- Write a letter to Jesus, by hand on a pretty sheet of paper.

- Focus on your invisible and often overlooked inner life. As you search your soul, ask your loving Heavenly Father to show you which attitudes, expectations, beliefs, or plans are holding you back from intimacy with Him.

- Identify your Spiritual Markers. Working in chronological order, make a list of all the major events in your life. Circle each event where you saw God clearly at work in your life. What did you learn about yourself and about God from each of your Markers?

- Be creative. Use your creative gifts to express your love for God. Play the piano. Sketch a portrait. Write a poem. Sew a garment. Whatever you do, do it in praise to the One who gave you your abilities.

- Create a photo journal. Take a walk in nature and snap photos of things that remind you of God. Later, create a slide show or photo book of the photos captioned with prayers of thanksgiving.

- Plan a personal retreat day, different from a day of solitude. Create a playlist of your favorite worship music, purchase a new CD, or purchase a new devotional for your retreat day. Select a location and place the date on your calendar. For this retreat, plan to engage in a different *Soul Nourishment* activity each hour. On the day of your personal retreat, set a timer to go off every hour. When the timer goes off, take a few minutes to connect with Jesus by listening to a worship song, reading part of the devotional, reciting a favorite Scripture passage, or talking with God before moving on to the next soul-nourishing activity.

6. The Ultimate Guide to Connecting with God

Contrary to popular belief, God did not create us all to worship Him in the same way. We are different not just in our physical appearance and spiritual giftedness but also in the way we connect with God. And it's a beautiful thing. One body, many parts, and lots of great ways to connect with the One True God through Jesus Christ.

The list below will provide some ideas for seeking God in new ways that may open up fresh paths of communication with Him. Use this guide to help discover the way God created YOU to connect with Him!

Naturalists Loving God Outdoors

- Go for a prayer walk around your neighborhood, praying for each neighbor individually by name.

- Rest. Take a nap. Thank God that He gives sleep to those He loves (Psalm 127:2).

- Read the Bible outside.

- Worship God while watching a sunrise or sunset; delight in His artistic expression and praise Him with each changing color.

- Read and memorize Bible verses that tell of nature declaring the glory of God (Psalm 19, 29; Job 38—41).

- Read poetry about how God reveals Himself in nature (i.e., Gerard Manley Hopkins' "God's Grandeur"); reflect on what you learn about God from these poems and how you can respond to Him.

- Lay down in the grass and look at the clouds, *the dust of God's feet* (Nahum 1:3); reflect on where God is moving and what He is doing in the world and in your life.

- Sing songs about God and nature (e.g., "All Creatures of our God and King;" "How Great Thou Art;" "In the Garden;" "Great Is Thy Faithfulness").

- Meditate on God's majesty while going on a hike; be inspired by the skies, the trees, and the rocks—if we do not praise Him, they will!

- Learn about macro and micro biology and astronomy, and worship God for how He created everything so meticulously and still cares for us.

Sensates Loving God with the Senses

- Listen to worship music from all different countries and get a preview of heaven where we will praise God with brothers and sisters from "every tribe and every tongue."

- Make up music for your favorite Scripture and sing it out loud.

- Light a candle during your devotions or use incense to engage your sense of smell in the act of worship.

- Absorb worship-producing art by meditating on God's truth as revealed in the arts (painting, sculpture, film, music, dance, etc.).

- Make art as an act of worship.

- If you play an instrument, have a private time of worship by playing for an audience of One.

- Pray in various positions: standing, sitting, kneeling, dancing, lying face-down, walking.

- Make one of your favorite snacks or beverages and share it with God while you talk about your day.

- Find local cathedrals open to the public and spend time in personal prayer there.

- When reading a Bible passage, imagine the scene in your mind: listen for the sea gulls, feel the scorching sun on your face, taste the fish, hear the thunder, smell the smoke...become one of the characters in the account and recreate the scene in your mind.

Traditionalists Loving God through Ritual and Symbol

- Read Scripture out loud.

- Use the Book of Common Prayer or Valley of Vision to guide your prayers.

- Meet with God at the same time and place every day.

- Study the history of the church to learn how God has been working throughout the ages.

- Read the Bible chronologically to gain a new understanding of how the events in the Bible fit together or pick one of many other Bible reading plans.

- Celebrate significant days in the church calendar like Lent, Pentecost, Advent, etc.

- Practice "prayer breaks" throughout the day, pausing for a few moments of prayer every hour. Set an alarm on your phone to help you remember.

- Read three chapters of the Bible a day, but don't stop there. Talk to God about what you read and what you have learned about Him in the text.

- Learn about the Jewish festivals and incorporate them in your yearly calendar.

- Study the creed and use it to reflect on how God has revealed Himself to us.

Ascetics Loving God in Solitude and Simplicity

- Rise up early in the morning for prayer, while it is dark and still.

- Create daily rhythms that center your heart on Jesus. This can include saying a prayer as soon as you open your eyes, reciting a specific passage each day as you dress, reading from a devotional book at every lunch, etc.

- Practice silence by not speaking AND by silencing the soundtrack in your mind.

- Fast from food and use meal times to pray.

- Clean out a closet and donate items to a relief organization.

- Practice "heart cleaning." Ask the Holy Spirit to reveal sins that you have harbored in your heart and repent of them.

- Practice solitude on a regular basis, getting away from people, phones, social media, and chores for a quiet respite to *be still, and know that [He is] God* (Psalm 46:10).

- Look around your house and bundle together any surplus you have to make basic care packets (shampoo, gloves, socks, oatmeal packets, nuts, etc.); give these to homeless people standing on street corners.

- Spend time on a night watch, staying up a portion (or all) of the night to focus on prayer, repentance, thanksgiving, and listening to God.

- Live on a tight budget and give the surplus to families in need and organizations you believe in.

Activists Loving God through Confrontation

- When you read or watch heart-breaking news, reflect on God's faithfulness despite the evils of the world and ask Him to comfort, strengthen, and intervene in the situation.

- Make a list of God's characteristics and over the course of a few days reflect on how each one has touched your life.

- Seek a woman older than you who can pray with you and talk you through seasons of your life.

- Research current legislature that is being discussed in your state and national congress. Pray for those issues as they come up for debate and vote.

- Serve Jesus at a local homeless shelter.

- Write a letter to your congressman asking for his/her intervention in the release and relief of persecuted Christians around the world. (For ideas of what to say, check out persecution.org.)

- Participate in campaigns that help rescue trafficked women and children, provide care for orphans, help widows support themselves, offer encouragement to terminally ill patients, etc.

- Pray for your city as you drive around running errands.

- Wherever you go, sit next to the loneliest person in the room and show them they are valued in Christ.

- Spend some time prayer-journaling what causes are heavy on your heart. Then research organizations that offer aid for those causes and prayerfully consider how you can get involved with others who are doing kingdom work.

Caregivers Loving God by Serving Others

- Open your home to students and love on them.

- Offer counseling and support at a local crisis pregnancy center.

- Visit elderly members of your church and ask them to tell you stories of God's faithfulness in their lives over some baked goods that you brought with you.

- Join a prayer team at your church and pray for the needs of your congregation.

- Volunteer to babysit your pastor's kids so he and his wife can have a date night.

- Pick a missionary family your church supports and get to know them. Send them birthday cards, small care packages, call them on Skype, pray for them, learn more about the culture they are living in, and look for practical ways to encourage them.

- Visit the hospital and seek out those patients who haven't received any visitors (flowers optional).

- Take a meal to a new mom or someone who is going through a long-term illness.

- Volunteer at an inner-city ministry.

- Write a letter of encouragement to a persecuted brother or sister in Christ who is imprisoned for their faith (you can check out Voice of the Martyrs for more information).

Enthusiasts Loving God with Mystery and Celebration

- Write down significant dreams and talk them over with God and someone you trust.

- Ask God each morning to bring someone across your path who needs you to minister to them.

- Say something nice to a stranger.

- Still your heart and listen to God; write down what you hear Him saying.

- Act out Bible stories with your children.

- Seek out a prayer partner and set a specific time and day each week to pray, whether together or apart.

- Take classes on theology, evangelism, counseling, etc.

- Serve in your church's nursery or children's department.

- Go through old picture albums and reflect on how God moved in different seasons of your life; think about people He used, conversations that drew you closer to Him, successes and failures, special events.

- Be the first to celebrate what God is doing in your life and in the lives of others by throwing dinner parties, writing cards of congratulations, sharing others' good news on social media (with their permission, of course), and dancing wildly around the house because of God's miracles.

Contemplatives Loving God through Adoration

- Use a short, set prayer to focus your mind on God.

- Read an account of Jesus' crucifixion from one of the gospels and slowly work through the scene in your mind; imagine the emotions of those present; picture the sights and smells; reflect on relevant prophesies Jesus fulfilled; end with a prayer of repentance, thanksgiving, and praise.

- Read a psalm and pray it personalized to you, by inserting "I" or your name.

- Pick a verse to meditate on while you close your eyes and breathe deeply.

- Keep pen and paper close to you while you pray and write down any stray thoughts or to-do items that come to mind so you can return your focus to God; before you finish your time of prayer, pray over each item you wrote down.

- Study artistic renditions of biblical scenes and meditate on that story. Use the passage to help you with details; identify emotions, expectations, and actions in the story. Reflect on God's character as revealed in the story and illuminated by the painting.

- Write down what comes to mind when you think about God; spend some time thanking Him for all the ways He cares and provides.

- Moving beyond what God does, take time to reflect on who He is. Read Scripture on His holiness, love, compassion, patience, righteousness, faithfulness, etc.

- Find a prayer warrior and spend time together in prayer. Focus your prayer time not on a list but on who God is and how He is working.

- Practice incorporating God's characteristics into your prayers. For example, when praying about job loss, thank God for being Jehovah Jirah, the One who provides, for taking care of you in the past, for giving daily bread and for being the Bread of Life, for knowing the future that is unknown to us, for already working at opening doors for you to walk through, for being ever-faithful, etc.

Intellectuals Loving God with the Mind

- Write down 15–20 observations on the Bible text you are reading. (The first few are easiest, but the last ones are the most rewarding.)

- Use a commentary when studying a passage to gain a broader understanding of the text.

GENERAL Soul Nourishment Resources

- Find other Christians who are interested in ethics and doctrine and discuss what you believe. Challenge each other to question presuppositions and to go deeper, but always with grace and truth.

- Read one book of the Bible at a time, studying a short paragraph a day to delve deep into the text.

- Take notes during the sermon and at the very end, identify one practical way to apply that day's teaching to your life that very day.

- Read books about the character of God (*The Knowledge of the Holy* by A. W. Tozer, *Knowing God* by J. I. Packer).

- Listen to podcasts or sermons while driving or working out.

- Pick a topic that interests you and spend a year studying it. Read each Bible reference, listen to sermons on it, read books on it, talk to others about it, write your thoughts on it, watch movies about it. Ask the Holy Spirit to teach you about that topic through events in your own life.

- Study the seven basic topics in systematic theology and know WHY you believe what you believe: God, humankind, Jesus, the Holy Spirit, the Church, eschatology, and revelation.

- Audit an online class at a Bible college you respect on a topic that interests you. Talk to God about what you are learning and seek ways to practice it in your life.

Introverts Loving God by Ourselves

- Write a letter of encouragement sharing what God is teaching you. If you do not know who to write to, ask the Holy Spirit to bring someone to mind.

- Use the minutes (or hours, for us insomniacs) before you fall asleep to pray for the people that God brings to mind.

- Divide your prayer requests into seven days of the week so you can pray for each request at least once a week.

- Identify a hope or fear in your life and pray about it every day for 40 days; repent of any sins He reveals to you on that topic; write down anything you sense God is telling you; do whatever He tells you to do; pray as the Spirit leads. At the end of the 40 days, reflect on what God has done and continue in prayer.

- Pray through the fruit of the Spirit, one each week. Ask God to cultivate that characteristic in you through specific events in your life that week (love, joy, peace, patience, kindness, goodness, faithfulness, gentleness, and self-control).

- Pray through a sketch of the temple, entering the gates with thanksgiving, thanking Jesus for being the showbread, asking God to wash you of your sins at the water basin, reflecting the sacrifice of the Lamb at the altar, and finally entering the Holy of Holies to stand in adoration of God.

- Read books by Christians who are not contemporaries; learn from ways God has revealed Himself to others in the past.

- Keep a list of daily blessings in your life.

- Find worship songs that put into words the thoughts of your heart, like "Be Thou My Vision," "Take My Life and Let It Be," "All to Jesus I Surrender."

- Practice talking to God throughout the day, making conversation about whatever it is you are doing, and asking for the Spirit's guidance in your actions.

Extroverts Loving God in Community with Others

- Keep a running list of prayer requests and each time you tell someone, "I'll pray for you," put them on the list. Then pray!

- Once a week, make dinner time story time. Tell your children and friends stories of how God has been faithful in your life and invite them to do the same.

- Follow up with people you have said you will pray for and ask them how God has been moving in their lives.

- Write down the story of your life, making note of the many ways God has provided for you and moved in different circumstances. Save it for your family to cherish once you have joined Jesus in heaven.

- Read the Bible in a short period of time, perhaps in four months, to get a birds-eye view of the entire storyline.

- While reading a Bible passage, interpret what you are reading by asking yourself: "What does this passage teach me about God? About myself? About the Christian life?"

- After reading a Bible passage, apply what you have read by identifying one action you will take that day in response to God's Word. Make it SMART: specific, measurable, attainable, realistic, and time-bound.

- Each night, share with your spouse or a friend at least one way God showed up that day.

- Read the Bible in community with other women.

- Offer to host a Bible study or prayer group in your home.

VAK (Visual, Auditory, and Kinesthetic) Loving God through Our Learning Styles

- Sketchnote your Bible readings by drawing pictures, using special fonts, and presenting what you are learning in a visual way. (visual)

- Journal your prayers like you are writing a letter to God. This helps focus. (visual)

- Write important verses on index cards and keep them around the house (or you can use premade ones). (visual)

- Listen to the Bible on tape or CD. (auditory)

- Read the Bible out loud, using intonation and expressions like you would while reading to a child. (auditory)

- Sing praise songs throughout your day, whether you are washing dishes, driving kids to school, or getting ready for bed. (auditory)

- Grab a cup of coffee or tea and have a conversation with Jesus. Out loud. (auditory)

- Build a physical model to remember God's faithfulness. Use items of significance from your past. (kinesthetic)

- Incorporate symbols you can touch and interact with into your prayer time. Symbols might include things such as a piece of jewelry, a prayer maze, or stations of the cross. Use the symbols to direct your heart toward God. (kinesthetic)

- Crochet or knit hats for the NICU at your local hospital, praying for the babies who will wear them and for their families. (kinesthetic)[32]

7. Ways to Feed Your Soul When You Are Busy with Life

1. Listen to the Bible
Download an app that will allow you to listen to the Bible while you are taking care of mundane chores. Other audio sources of the Bible are CDs, DVDs, and links through online Bible sites.

2. Pray as You Work
Think about your day. Much of our normal activity provides plenty of opportunity for prayer: waiting in line at the grocery, sitting in the carpool line, doing the dishes, cleaning the kitchen, folding laundry, scrubbing the bathrooms, dusting, weeding. Where can you pray as you work?

3. Provide a Soundtrack for Your Work
Listen to podcasts of sermons from your church or a favorite pastor while cooking dinner or cleaning up the kitchen. Choose praise music to fit your mood or to focus your heart and mind. You might select some upbeat praise music while performing routine daily tasks. Consider building a playlist of cross-centered songs to turn your heart toward God.

4. Invest in Christian Friendships
We were made for community by the creator of the universe. By His design, we need each other. Invest in life-giving relationship with soul friends. Develop a history together, celebrate your strengths, offer encouragement in weakness. Share life, all of it, the big and the small. Go for coffee, enjoy play dates, study the Bible together, pray. Most importantly, be honest. Share your struggles and your failures. Vulnerability is hard, but growth is in the hard places. And life is in the receiving of acceptance and grace from one who is FOR you.

5. Write Scripture by Hand
Even if only one verse of Scripture a day, take the time to write out Scripture by hand. Use a small journal or composition book and write out one verse each day. If you are a "calendar/planner" person, write out your verse directly into your daily planner. The process only takes a few minutes but reaps powerful benefits as it slows you down to see the detail within the Scripture.

6. Meditate on Scripture

We have almost completely lost the art of biblical meditation. Fill your mind with the truths of God's Word. Set a meditation alarm on your phone. When it goes off, pull out your hand-written verse of the day and meditate on it. Post Scripture on your bathroom mirror or refrigerator. Decorate your home with the Word of God. Surround yourself with the words of Scripture: read them, meditate on them, memorize them.

7. Memorize Scripture

Scripture memorization is absolutely fundamental to soul care. Hiding God's Word in our heart helps us grow to be more like Jesus, guards against sin, and is one of the most effective ways to meditate on Scripture. Write it out by hand, say it out loud, pray it, sing it, draw it, photograph it.

8. Practice His Presence

Where shall I go from your Spirit?
Or where shall I flee from your presence?
If I ascend to heaven, you are there!
If I make my bed in Sheol, you are there!

Psalm 139:7-8

God's presence is with us. It is IN us. A powerful truth for the believer in Christ, but one that is so often not acknowledged. Practice His Presence. Spend time with Him daily. Carry on conversations with Him. Set an alarm to go off several times throughout your day as a reminder to be with Him.

Participating

Or do you not know that your body is a temple
of the Holy Spirit within you, whom you have from God?
You are not your own, for you were bought with a price.
So glorify God in your body.

1 Corinthians 6:19-20

God alone creates. Scripture opens with the account of God creating a perfectly ordered dwelling place for His presence. And the final scene recorded in Revelation 21 describes His reordering of a fallen world, unveiling the New Jerusalem, a perfectly ordered dwelling place for His presence. Between these bookend accounts, the Old Testament records several instances of God inviting humans into the process of creating a perfectly ordered dwelling place for His presence (the building of the tabernacle in Exodus, the building of Solomon's Temple in 1 Kings, the rebuilding of Jerusalem in Ezra and Nehemiah). As temples of the Holy Spirit, we are called to be participants in the process of creating and maintaining within our hearts the place for His presence. Practice participating in the creation of a space where heaven and earth (divine and human) can commune together.

Partnering

Iron sharpens iron, and one man sharpens another.

Proverbs 27:17

Engage fellow disciples of Jesus in prayerful conversation or other spiritual practices. Set up regular and consistent Partnering appointments. During your time together, pray, read Scripture, ask each other accountability questions, Bible journal, enjoy a worship concert or Bible conference. And don't forget to encourage one another in the days in between.

Paying Attention

Have you not known? Have you not heard?
The Lord is the everlasting God,
the Creator of the ends of the earth.
He does not faint or grow weary;
his understanding is unsearchable.

Isaiah 40:28

Pay Attention. Slow down. Lean in. Give reverence to God by Paying Attention to Him and to others. Turn off the devices, turn your focus toward the one you are with, and physically lean in.

Peace & Quiet

And after he had dismissed the crowds, he went up on the mountain by himself to pray. When evening came, he was there alone,

Matthew 14:23

You are designed by God for times of Peace and Quiet. Get away from the noise and away from the distractions regularly. Schedule an hour each week or an entire day once a month, but put this time on your calendar. Nourish your soul in quiet alone time with God, your Father.

Perceiving

I give you good precepts;
do not forsake my teaching.

Proverbs 4:2

The Bible has been given to us and preserved these many years for our benefit. Yes, read it for pleasure letting its words wash over you, but don't stop there. The Bible is filled with good precepts for our learning. Slow your reading down and perceive. Write Scripture out by hand. Engage with His Word. See the details.

Place

"Be still, and know that I am God.
I will be exalted among the nations,
I will be exalted in the earth!"

Psalm 46:10 (ESV)

One of the names for God in Hebrew Scriptures is *Ha-Makom* meaning "the omnipresent." Literally translated, it is "The Place." It is interesting to note that the traditional Jewish sentiment offered to someone in grief contains this very name for God. "*HaMakom yenachem et 'chem*" means "May The Place comfort you." We so often feel that we are without a place, but God is The Place. He is always with us. Be with Him.

Plenty

Not that I am speaking of being in need,
for I have learned in whatever situation I am to be content.

Philippians 4:11

Plenty means "fullness, a full supply, more than sufficient." No matter the current circumstance, even when there seems to be very little or that things are going to run out, Plenty can be found. Plenty of love, family, friendship, laughter, hope, beauty…. Look for it. It is there. Record the Plenty in words or in photographs.

Praise

Therefore, as you received Christ Jesus the Lord, so walk in him, rooted and built up in him and established in the faith, just as you were taught, abounding in thanksgiving.

Colossians 2:6-7

Practice Praise by offering gratitude and thanksgiving unto God at all times and in all things. Thank God for three things each night before going to sleep. List ten things you are thankful for in your journal each day. Fold the laundry to praise music.

Prayer

Continue steadfastly in prayer.

Colossians 4:2

Prayer is a way of life, an ongoing conversation with God. Pray when you are all alone. Pray with others. Breathe breath prayers, pray passages of Scripture, or utter a single word. Sketch your prayers, write them down, pray A through Z.

Pondering

But Mary treasured up all these things, pondering them in her heart.

Luke 2:19

Mary, the mother of Jesus, practiced Pondering. In the Greek, the word means "to bring together; place together for comparison." Mary Pondered it all: the prophetic words of the Old Testament, the words of the angel Gabriel, Elizabeth's words, the words of the shepherds. Mary watched and listened, holding each new unfolding to the light and comparing it with the pieces she already held. Rearranging. Considering again. Make a practice of Pondering. Record life's happenings in a journal. Ask questions. Look again at each piece. Compare them to one another. Reflect on what you notice.

Position

*And raised us up with him and seated us with him
in the heavenly places in Christ Jesus,*

Ephesians 2:6

Believers in Christ are "seated." We don't have to fight for a seat. We already have one "with him in the heavenly places!" We can stop wrangling for recognition, longing to fit in, and comparing ourselves to everyone else. We can begin loving out of the overflow of love the King lavishes on us, rejoice with others in their successes, relax in our "seating," and abide. Spend some time with Ephesians 2:1-10 and practice your Position.

Prizing

*Oh, magnify the Lord with me,
and let us exalt his name together!*

Psalm 34:3

And Mary said, "My soul magnifies the Lord" (Luke 1:46). Mary prized the Lord and offered her song as an act of worship. Take the time to practice Prizing. Offer gifts of worship. Share your God-story with others, notice His creativity, sing songs of praise, list His attributes A through Z, then offer the list back to Him in prayer.

9. Tips for Dealing with Distractions

Prepare Ahead
If you enjoy morning quiet times, prepare for them the night before by getting all of your materials ready.

Scout Out a Well-Suited Location
Choose a spot that is as free from distraction as possible.

Turn Off the Technology
Before settling down, be sure your phone is silenced. Consider physically removing yourself from things like phones, iPads, computers, and TVs.

Tune Out the Noise
If it is not possible to move to a location with zero to minimal noise distraction, try using ear plugs or noise-cancelling headphones.

Keep a Note Pad Handy
As things pop into your mind, simply write them down. Acknowledge the distractions, jot them down, and return your attention to your quiet time.

Take a Walk
Fresh air and exercise are always good. But walking as you pray, reflect, or meditate on Scripture engages your body and helps to keep you focused. Go for a walk at your nearby park, prayer walk around your neighborhood, or walk your yard. If you can't get outside, try walking through your home or pacing.

Hydrate
It is difficult to focus when our body has needs. Make yourself comfortable before you begin. Take care of your needs.

Check Your Posture
Before entering your quiet time, take a few minutes to properly posture yourself before the Lord. Get comfortable but not too comfortable. Take a couple of deep breaths and consciously let go of tasks and responsibilities. Try observing a few moments of silence before beginning. Picture yourself seated across the table from God.

Prepare Your Heart
Consider beginning your time with some "nobody's home, belt-it-out" singing!

Get a New Perspective
Try reading your chosen passage of Scripture from an unfamiliar translation of the Bible. Wording differences, even subtle ones, require focused attention.

Talk to Yourself
We are pretty good at paying attention to ourselves. Combat quiet time distractions by reading Scripture aloud, rephrasing what you read, repeating truths you are learning, or talking through what you are wrestling with.

Pray Out Loud
It may feel uncomfortable at first, but there are a couple of benefits to praying out loud. First, it is more difficult for your mind to wander off aimlessly when you pray out loud. The other benefit? It is not possible for Satan to read our minds. When we pray out loud, Satan can hear it!!

Combine the Spiritual Practices
Combine reading the Bible with prayer to pray Scripture. Do some serious soul-reflecting while observing a time of solitude. Journal your prayers or Scripture study.

Make the Fight Personal
- Commit.
- Create a distraction plan.
  - › Consider your unique God-created wiring.
  - › Give yourself permission to tweak your plan.
  - › If you need or enjoy variety, build it into your plan.
- Establish check points along the way.
  - › Revisit your plan regularly—once a year, every six months, or quarterly.
  - › Life season change, distraction plans may need to change along with our season.
- Give yourself the grace to readjust the plan when needed and to keep going.

Prayer

SOUL NOURISHMENT RESOURCES

10. How to Pray: A Biblical Guide to Prayer

Continue steadfastly in prayer, being watchful in it with thanksgiving.
Colossians 4:2

"Lord, teach us to pray" (Luke 11:1).

- And God heard [Jesus'] prayers because of His **deep reverence** for God (Hebrews 5:7, NLT).
- Let us come to Him **with thanksgiving** (Psalm 95:2, NLT).
- So let us come boldly **to the throne** of our gracious God (Hebrews 4:16, NLT).
- But when you ask Him, be sure that your **faith is in God alone** (James 1:6, NLT).

Our Father which art in heaven, Hallowed be thy name (Matthew 6:9, KJV).

- loving
- just
- eternal
- infinite
- wise
- good
- merciful
- sustainer
- righteous
- jealous
- creator
- everywhere
- sovereign
- gracious
- all powerful

Thy kingdom come, Thy will be done in earth, as it is in heaven (Matthew 6:10, KJV).

- **Trust** in the LORD **with all your heart**, and do not lean on your own understanding. In all your ways **acknowledge him**, and he will make straight your paths (Proverbs 3:5–6).

Give us this day our daily bread. And forgive us our debts... (Matthew 6:11–12, KJV).

- The LORD is near to all who call on him, to all who call on him in truth (Psalm 145:18).
- **Pray** in the Spirit; in Jesus Name; in faith in the power of the Holy Spirit (1 Corinthians 14:15, John 14:13, Mark 11:24, Jude 1:20).
- **Keep on** asking, seeking, and knocking (Luke 11:9).
- **Always pray** and never give up (Luke 18:1).
- **Pray for** all people; for those in authority; for people to be saved; for a clean heart and a loyal spirit; for salvation; for the suffering; for your worries; for the things

you need; for God's mercy; for a clear conscience; in your troubles; to not give in to temptation; for enemies; for all believers everywhere; that the Son can bring glory to the Father; for God's will to be done; in thanksgiving; for healing (I Timothy 2:1–2, Romans 10:1, Psalm 51:10, 2 Chronicles 7:14, James 5:13–14, Philippians 4:6, Psalm 4:1, Hebrews 13:18, Matthew 26:41, Romans 12:14, Ephesians 6:18, John 14:13, Matthew 6:10, Psalm 95:2).

...as we forgive our debtors. And lead us not into temptation, but deliver us from evil: For thine is the kingdom, and the power, and the glory, for ever. Amen (Matthew 6:12–13, KJV).[33]

Adapted from *How to Pray: A Biblical Guide to Prayer* Infographic by Ben Griffin.

11. How to Pray for the Soul

- **An inclination to God and His word.** *Incline my heart to your testimonies, and not to selfish gain!* (Psalm 119:36).

- **Open the eyes of my heart.** *Open my eyes, that I may behold wondrous things out of your law* (Psalm 119:18).

- **Enlighten my heart to Your wonders.** *[H]aving the eyes of your hearts enlightened, that you may know what is the hope to which he has called you, what are the riches of his glorious inheritance in the saints* (Ephesians 1:18).

- **That my heart be united for God.** *Teach me your way, O Lord, that I may walk in your truth; unite my heart to fear your name* (Psalm 86:11).

- **That my heart will be satisfied with God and not with the world.** *Satisfy us in the morning with your steadfast love, that we may rejoice and be glad all our days* (Psalm 90:14).

- **I will be strong in joy and durable in the face of adversity.** *[T]hat according to the riches of his glory he may grant you to be strengthened with power through his Spirit in your inner being* (Ephesians 3:16).

- **That my strength in Christ produce good deeds so that He will be glorified.** *[S]o as to walk in a manner worthy of the Lord, fully pleasing to him, bearing fruit in every good work and increasing in the knowledge of God* (Colossians 1:10).

- **For God to be glorified.** *Pray then like this: "Our Father in heaven, hallowed be your name"* (Matthew 6:9).

- **In Jesus' name.** *He who did not spare his own Son but gave him up for us all, how will he not also with him graciously give us all things?* (Romans 8:32).[34]

12. Tips for Praying Scripture

- Designate a specific place.

- As much as possible, eliminate distractions.

- Before you begin, quiet your mind and invite the Holy Spirit into your time of prayer.

- Pray the meaning of the passage not just the words.

- Pray thoughtfully—contemplate, meditate, reflect.

- Read the passage in context.

- Search out the author of the passage, the audience, the culture, etc.

- Write out your prayers. Include the date.

- Write out the Scriptures by hand. Post them in visible areas around your home or carry them with you. Throughout the day, read them as prayers.

- Create a Scripture Prayer Journal. Section your journal off by topic—prayers for family, prayers for personal growth, prayers for comfort, prayers of praise, etc. Collect Scriptures to pray by writing them in the appropriate section of your journal. Pull out your journal when you feel the need for prayer in a certain area.

13. Pray Scripture

Pray the Psalms

Any portion of Scripture can be prayed. However, if you need a good starting or getting-unstuck place, try the book of Psalms.

Choose any Psalm you like and read through it thoughtfully, personalize it by inserting your own name, or respond to it as you read.

Having difficulty choosing a Psalm? Here's an old tried and true method: Select a numbered Psalm that corresponds to the current day of the month.

Day 1 – Psalm 1, Psalm 31, Psalm 61, Psalm 91, or Psalm 121

Day 2 – Psalm 2, Psalm 32, Psalm 62, Psalm 92, or Psalm 122

Day 3 – Psalm 3, Psalm 33, Psalm 63, Psalm 93, or Psalm 123

Day 4 – Psalm 4, Psalm 34, Psalm 64, Psalm 94, or Psalm 124

Day 5 – Psalm 5, Psalm 35, Psalm 65, Psalm 95, or Psalm 125

Day 6 – Psalm 6, Psalm 36, Psalm 66, Psalm 96, or Psalm 126

Day 7 – Psalm 7, Psalm 37, Psalm 67, Psalm 97, or Psalm 127

Day 8 – Psalm 8, Psalm 38, Psalm 68, Psalm 98, or Psalm 128

Day 9 – Psalm 9, Psalm 39, Psalm 69, Psalm 99, or Psalm 129

Day 10 – Psalm 10, Psalm 40, Psalm 70, Psalm 100, or Psalm 130

Day 11 – Psalm 11, Psalm 41, Psalm 71, Psalm 101, or Psalm 131

Day 12 – Psalm 12, Psalm 42, Psalm 72, Psalm 102, or Psalm 132

Day 13 – Psalm 13, Psalm 43, Psalm 73, Psalm 103, or Psalm 133

Day 14 – Psalm 14, Psalm 44, Psalm 74, Psalm 104, or Psalm 134

Day 15 – Psalm 15, Psalm 45, Psalm 75, Psalm 105, or Psalm 135

Day 16 – Psalm 16, Psalm 46, Psalm 76, Psalm 106, or Psalm 136

Day 17 – Psalm 17, Psalm 47, Psalm 77, Psalm 107, or Psalm 137

Day 18 – Psalm 18, Psalm 48, Psalm 78, Psalm 108, or Psalm 138

Day 19 – Psalm 19, Psalm 49, Psalm 79, Psalm 109, or Psalm 139

Day 20 – Psalm 20, Psalm 50, Psalm 80, Psalm 110, or Psalm 140

Day 21 – Psalm 21, Psalm 51, Psalm 81, Psalm 111, or Psalm 141

Day 22 – Psalm 22, Psalm 52, Psalm 82, Psalm 112, or Psalm 142

Day 23 – Psalm 23, Psalm 53, Psalm 83, Psalm 113, or Psalm 143

Day 24 – Psalm 24, Psalm 54, Psalm 84, Psalm 114, or Psalm 144

Day 25 – Psalm 25, Psalm 55, Psalm 85, Psalm 115, or Psalm 145

Day 26 – Psalm 26, Psalm 56, Psalm 86, Psalm 116, or Psalm 146

Day 27 – Psalm 27, Psalm 57, Psalm 87, Psalm 117, or Psalm 147

Day 28 – Psalm 28, Psalm 58, Psalm 88, Psalm 118, or Psalm 148

Day 29 – Psalm 29, Psalm 59, Psalm 89, Psalm 119, or Psalm 149

Day 30 – Psalm 30, Psalm 60, Psalm 90, Psalm 120, or Psalm 150

Day 31 – Choose any Psalm or read Psalm 119

REMEMBER: Praying Scripture is all about engaging with Scripture and conversing with your Heavenly Father. Don't overwhelm yourself by taking on too much and trying to pray through all five chapters each day. Choose one, any one, and spend your time there.

14. Praying in Color

Praying in Color = prayer + doodling

What you need:
- Paper
- Pen, Sharpie, black roller ball pen
- Colored markers, colored pencils, colored gel pens
- A surface to work on

How to get started:
1. Write the name of the person you are praying for on a piece of paper. Draw a shape around it or just start to doodle.

2. Add marks and shapes. Focus on the person. Ask God to be part of your prayer time. If words come, pray them; if not, enjoy the silence.

3. Choose a character virtue, Scripture, specific need, or anything else to pray for that person. Write it in another area of your paper. Pray as you draw around it, adding color and doodles.

4. Continue to add other virtues, Scriptures, or specifics to your "prayer." Pray for each as it pertains to the person. As you pray, add color and doodles.[35]

Praying in Color can be adapted to any type of prayer: thanksgiving, intercessory, praise, or adoration. It can also be used as you spend time with a Scripture verse or passage.

Financial Struggle   Being a Parent   Asking for Help   Patience

Freedom   SYLVIA   Love Joy

In Him and through faith in Him we may approach God with freedom and confidence. Ephesians 3:12

15. Contemplative Prayer

And after the earthquake a fire, but the L*ord* *was not in the fire.*
And after the fire the sound of a low whisper.

1 Kings 19:12

....

[T]that the God of our Lord Jesus Christ, the Father of glory,
may give you the Spirit of wisdom and of revelation in the knowledge of him,
having the eyes of your hearts enlightened, that you may know
what is the hope to which he has called you.

Ephesians 1:17-18

Contemplation is done with the "eyes of your heart." It is, in other words, spiritual "seeing."

1. Draw away to a quiet place.

2. Pray. Invite the Holy Spirit into this time with you. Ask Him to open the "eyes of your heart."

3. Thoughtfully read a passage of Scripture.

4. As you read: pause, lean in, look closely, pray.

5. Reflect on what you have "seen."

6. Close in prayer. Respond to what you have read. Thank God for the biblical truths He has revealed or reaffirmed to you.[36]

16. Breath Prayers from Scripture

Short. Easy. Simple prayers that can be spoken in a single breath and repeated numerous times throughout the day. Cultivating the habit of breath prayers enables you to *pray without ceasing* (1 Thessalonians 5:17).

Choose a brief sentence or a simple phrase that you can repeat in one breath. Pray that sentence or phrase as often as possible during your day so that it becomes rooted deep in your heart.

- "Speak Lord, for your servant hears" (1 Samuel 3:9, 10, NKJV).

- "The Lord is my shepherd; I shall not want" (Psalm 23:1).

- "Be still, and know that I am God" (Psalm 46:10).

- *When I am afraid, I put my trust in you* (Psalm 56:3).

- "I will give thanks to you, O Lord" (Psalm 57:9, 108:3).

- *In Christ alone my soul finds rest…Selah* (Based on Psalm 62:1, 5).

- *My help comes from the Lord, who made heaven and earth* (Psalm 121:2).

- *Lord, have mercy* (Psalm 123:3, Luke 18:13, and Luke 18:38).

- *His steadfast love endures forever* (Psalm 136).

- "Here I am!" (Isaiah 6:8).

- *Peace! Be still!* (Mark 4:39).

- "Not my will, but yours" (Luke 22:42).

- "Your Kingdom come" (Luke 11:2).

- *To live is Christ, and to die is gain* (Philippians 1:21).

- *Come, Lord Jesus!* (Revelation 22:20).

17. When You Just Can't Pray

- Listen.

- Simply sit with Jesus.

- Utter His name.

- Breathe breath prayers.

- Offer praise.

- Ask God for help.

- Pray Scripture.

- Pray in Color using no words.

- Ask a soul friend to pray for you.

- Keep an ongoing list of things for which you are thankful.

Engaging with Scripture

SOUL NOURISHMENT RESOURCES

18. Ten Ways to Immerse Yourself in Scripture

1. Read it.
Read it in the privacy of your home all curled up in your favorite spot, or read it together with a friend or two. Read it for pleasure letting its words cascade over you, or get down to business and read it with a pen. Don't worry about how much you are reading. It really doesn't matter if it's an entire book, two chapters, or simply a verse or two. What's much more important is what you are learning and how you are growing in Christ.

2. Listen to the Bible.
It can be pretty difficult to hold a Bible in your lap while children are climbing all over you or you are folding laundry. Pull up an audio version and listen to the words of Scripture when you aren't able to read them.

3. Write Scripture out by hand.
The physical act of writing is good for the brain and great penmanship practice. It also helps us slow down and enables us to see detail we would not otherwise see. For fun make your writings "cute" by using creative lettering or fancy little doodles and then post them around your home.

4. Hang Scripture art in your home.
Have a family verse? Make it into a poster! Buy a piece of art that really captures the heart and soul of your family. Create a wall of truth centered around a biblical theme. Vinyl wall decals are also a very inexpensive way to implement Scripture art into your home decor.

5. Build Scripture playlists.
Create soundtracks for your life. Choose a theme, mood, or tempo. There are so many possibilities. Your library might contain a cross-centered day list, a classic hymns list, a list to play while dusting or vacuuming, an accompaniment to Bible journaling time, or an after dinner list.

6. Double dip.
Listen to Scripture music as a means for memorizing Scripture. Music is one of the easiest methods for this often dreaded task!

7. Preach truth to yourself.
Are there certain things that seem to send you into the land of negativity? Rather than allowing yourself to get caught up in negative self-talk and all the ugly feelings that can follow, post Scripture truths around your home. When those thoughts begin to roll, stop. Put your eyes on the truth of God's Word posted right there in your home and be reminded.

8. Carry Scripture with you.
Our homes aren't the only place where we need to preach Scripture to ourselves. Carry Scripture cards (either purchased or hand-written) with you in your car, purse, or bag. Use Scripture wallpapers for the home screens of your electronic devices.

9. Make good use of your wait times.
Whether it's a physical copy of Scripture or an online app, pull it out to read whenever you find yourself waiting—in the parent pickup line, in the doctor's waiting room, while the car is being repaired, in the checkout lane, or while the kids are at practice.

10. Pray Scripture.
Select a simple verse, perhaps one of the Scripture breath prayers. Set the alarm on your phone to go off at multiple times throughout your day. Each time the alarm goes off, pray that simple Scripture prayer.

19. Read the Bible with Focus

- Read, read, and read some more. The same passage over several days.
- Substitute your name for personal pronouns.
- Highlight things that jump out at you.
- Look for repeated words, phrases, or ideas.
- Search for patterns.
- Look for key words.
- Break down words.
- Look up synonyms.
- Look up word definitions.
- Connect words.
- Make a list.
- Draw a picture.
- Identify imagery and symbols.
- Ask questions.
- Look for if/then relationships.
- Locate cause and effect.
- If there is a "therefore," ask what it's there for.
- Cross reference.
- Find supporting Scripture.
- Find a question and answer it.
- Rephrase the Scripture using your own words.
- Summarize.
- Use tools: dictionaries, cross-references, commentaries, online Bible sites.
- Write about it. Start a Scripture journal.
- Discuss it with someone else.
- Look for things that please God.
- Make application to your daily life.
- Look for doctrine or a principle and relate it to a situation in your current season of life.
- Look for gospel principles illustrated by people, places, or events.
- Connect to a hymn or song.
- Memorize it.
- Meditate on it.
- Pray it.
- Connect to something in everyday life.
- Look for strategies on how to overcome attacks of Satan.
- Ask what the passage teaches you about God.

20. Bible Study Methods

Choose a method that fits your purpose, personality, mood, or current available amount of time.

Study the Bible by Book

- **Gather Background.** Learn what you can about the author of the book, when and where it was written, to whom, and why.

- **Read, Read, Read, and Read Some More.** Get the big picture. Begin by reading all the way through the book in one sitting. Do this several times.

- **Take Note.** In your notebook write out the themes and style of the book. Create a list of key words and verses as well. Want to know more? Look up word definitions and cross-references.

- **Create an Outline.** Old-school, yes, but quite effective. Work through the book point by point.

- **Make Application.** Reflect. Pray. Determine how the truths revealed in this book apply to you.

Study the Bible by Character

- **Gather Background Information.** Use your cross references and concordance. Find all the verses you can about this Bible character.

- **Frame a Quick Character Sketch.** From your texts, make note of any basic information you uncover regarding your character. Also, be sure to jot down your first impressions.

- **Make a Timeline.** Outline the person's life in chronological order. Don't dwell on details. Simply list events.

- **Dig Deeper.** Get to know the character. Delve into their relationships, actions, responses, reputation, and private life.

- **Prepare a Character Sketch.** Make a list of the character qualities you uncover over your numerous readings. List them all, the good and the bad. Be sure to record Scripture references for each.

- **Pull It All Together.** Look back at your notes and examine this character's life. What lessons can be learned? What biblical truths are revealed? In your notebook, write out a short summary of what you learned.

- **Make Application.** Reflect. Pray. Ask God to help you determine how the truths revealed in this book apply to you.

Study the Bible by Topic

- **Select Your Topic.** Decide on a topic of study. Choose something of high interest to you right now in this season of life.

- **Dig In.** Gather Bible verses and passages on your topic. Use your Bible's concordance, an online Bible site, or a google search for help.

- **Observe.** Read each verse and passage you have collected. Always read the references in context to help you gain a more accurate understanding of what is being said. Ask the important questions: Who? What? When? Where? Why? And how? Make note of what you discover.

- **Examine.** Compare the texts. Can any of them be grouped together? Do the groupings lead to an organized arrangement? Create an idea map or an outline of your topic with your findings.

- **Make Application.** What biblical truths have you learned from your study of the topic? Reflect. Pray. Ask God to help you determine how the truths revealed in this book apply to you.

21. Five Ways to Enhance Bible Study Time

1. Pray

- Begin with prayer. Invite the Holy Spirit into your time of reading. Seek guidance and understanding. Ask God to open your spiritual eyes, to soften your heart, and to reveal His truths.

- Pray as you read. Ask for clarification, seek repentance, offer thanksgiving.

- End with prayer. Pray in response to what you read and what you learned.

2. Know the Context

Before you read a passage, do your homework. Knowledge of the context provides better understanding. Answer these questions: Who wrote it? To whom was it written? Why was it written? When was it written? What is the historical context? What was the culture? Look for the information in your Bible (book introductions, notes, or indexes) or do an Internet search.

3. Read with Focus

There is a time and place for pleasure reading of the Bible; however, when study is the purpose, reading must be done with focus. It's much like preparing a research paper for school. Enter your reading time with much anticipation and ready to work. Read and re-read, highlight, circle, make note, mull it over.

Focus your entire attention on what you are reading—put away the phone, computer, food, and anything else that could possibly distract you. Find a place in your home and make it your study nook—the place where your brain automatically knows that it is God time. True growth happens in the times of focused reading.

4. Break It Down

- Use your English dictionary. Clarify the meaning of words by looking them up. Another great tool to use is a thesaurus. Look up synonyms.

- Go back and scrutinize these words in light of their surrounding context.

- Pay attention to the phrasing of the passage. Notice word tense.

- Ask questions.

    › What is the emphasis of the author?
    › What is the author trying to teach?
    › What does this passage reveal about God?
    › What do I learn about myself?
    › How will I respond?

5. Write Everything Down

When you study the Bible, keep a journal next to you. Develop a habit of writing down all the things God is teaching you as you read and study. Don't trust your memory. It is so easy to forget—even the things that seem to make a huge impact in the moment.

Write it all out in great detail or jot it down bullet point style. List key words or sketch what made an impact. Illustrate main points with stickers and stamped images. Play around with this step to see what best works for you! The bottom-line is to record what stands out to you from your time with the Lord and to do it in a meaningful way.

This method might sound time consuming; but remember that good things take time. So take it slowly. Read one chapter a day or even one verse a day. Write it down. Spend hours thinking about what you read. Record your thoughts. Pray about what you read. Go beyond the simple calling out of words on a page. The greater benefit comes from the time spent engaging.

> This Book of the Law shall not depart from your mouth, but you shall meditate on it day and night, so that you may be careful to do according to all that is written in it. For then you will make your way prosperous, and then you will have good success.
>
> Joshua 1:8

22. Lectio Divina

Lectio Divina is a traditional method of Bible reading and prayer, which literally translates to "sacred reading."

How to Practice Lectio Divina (One Approach)

Reading: What does the text say? First, read the text. At the most basic level, ask: What is going on in this Bible passage? Sometimes a Bible commentary is helpful to enable you to better understand the context.

Meditation: What is God saying to me through the text? At this point, ask whether there is something that God might want to reveal to you through this passage. Often, it might connect with something in your life.

Prayer: What do I want to say to God about the text? Tell God about your feelings. Be honest— don't worry: God can handle any emotions you have!

Action: What do I want to do, based on my prayer? Finally, act. Prayer should move us to action, even if it simply makes us want to be more compassionate and faithful.

Lectio Divina (Another Approach)

Choose a text of the Scriptures you wish to pray or study.

Turn to the text and read it slowly, gently. Read it several times, savoring the Word. Listen for a word that says, "I am for you today." Do not expect thunder or lightning. Sometimes a word will jump out at you; sometimes not. Ponder the word; think on it. Look it up in a dictionary or thesaurus.

Talk with God about the word and about what it has to teach you about truth, His Word, His character, your relationship with Him. Interact with God. Pray silently, pray aloud, or pray in color. Give to Him anything you have discovered during your time with Him and His Word. Give to God what you have found within your heart.

Rest in God's embrace.

Sometimes in *Lectio Divina*, you may return several times to the printed text, either to savor the literary context of the word or phrase that God has given or to seek a new word or phrase to ponder. At other times, only a single word or phrase will fill the whole time set aside for *Lectio Divina*. It is not necessary to assess anxiously the quality of your *Lectio*

Divina, as if you were "performing" or seeking some goal. *Lectio Divina* has no goal other than that of being in the presence of God by praying the Scriptures.

Variations

Audio Divina
(literally, "sacred listening")

Audio Divina enables you to listen to the Scripture instead of reading it. Websites dedicated to *Audio Divina* can be found through a quick Google search.

Visio Divina
(literally, "sacred seeing")

While *Lectio Divina* is a method of praying with scripture, *Visio Divina* is a method for praying with images or other media. (This process can be done at your computer, in a museum, with a book of images, anywhere you have access to images.) A quick look through Scripture will give indication to the importance God places on the use of images as a means of communication. Take for example, Ezekiel's vision of dry bones and Peter's dream on the rooftop in Acts chapter ten. Both are illustrations of the vital connection between images and prayer.

23. Verse Mapping

Verse Mapping is a method for familiarizing yourself with a verse. It is a way to really digest Scripture. Verse Mapping is a simple method that can be done by anyone regardless of their maturity in the faith. Parents, if your children are old enough, invite them to work on the same verse with you! At dinner, have everyone get out the card(s) and share as family how God has spoken through His Word that day.

Step 1
Gather your supplies. You will need an index card, sheet of paper, or blank journal page. You will also need your Bible and a pen. Feel free to use any color you want! Optional: English dictionary, concordance, online Bible help sites.

Step 2
Ask God to share with you a verse He would like you to focus on for the day. You can find one in a variety of ways.

- Bible Study: Use any verse from your current Bible study.

- Bible Cracking: Close your Bible, open it to a random page, and point to a verse.

- Concordance {Index}: Use the one in the back of your Bible or use an online source such as Bible Gateway or Blue Letter Bible. Look up a specific word or topic that God is laying on your heart. From the Bible references pertaining to that word or topic, choose a verse.

- Ask a Friend: Ask someone you know is close with God to recommend a verse.

- Devotions: Perhaps in the devotion you read in the morning, a verse jumps out at you. Use it for the day!

Step 3
Write out your verse by hand on your sheet of paper. Space it out as you write. Leave plenty of room around the verse and between the lines.

Step 4
Use the suggestions on the following page to map your verse.

Step 5
Close your time in prayer. Meditate on your verse throughout the day. Before going to bed at the end of the day, take one final look at the verse. If you still have room, write a little prayer sharing with God what you have learned.

Ideas and Suggestions for Mapping (Step 4)

- Personalize it—cross out words like "you," "we," "whoever," "them" and write *your* name above it.

- Highlight parts that jump out at you.

- Read the verse in context—the whole chapter or passage.

- Read the verse in at least two other translations. Note on the card words or phrases from other translations that help you understand or apply the verse. If you don't have other translations laying around the house, a couple of good resources for several translations are Bible Gateway, Blue Letter Bible, and YouVersion.

- Find cross references and note anything that brings new meaning. Cross references are verses that have similar words or phrases. Some Bibles list cross references in the center column; others in the footnotes. Again, Bible Gateway, Blue Letter Bible, and YouVersion can be of help.

- Circle a word or two and do a word study.
    › Look up the word in your dictionary and see if the definition gives you any insight.
    › Use a topical index and/or concordance in the back of your Bible to find other verses where the word appears.
    › Look up synonyms (same meaning) and antonyms (opposite meaning) in a concordance or online Bible tools site to find other verses.

- Write out what you are learning.

- Record your thoughts on how you can apply the Scripture to your daily living.

Verse Mapping Example

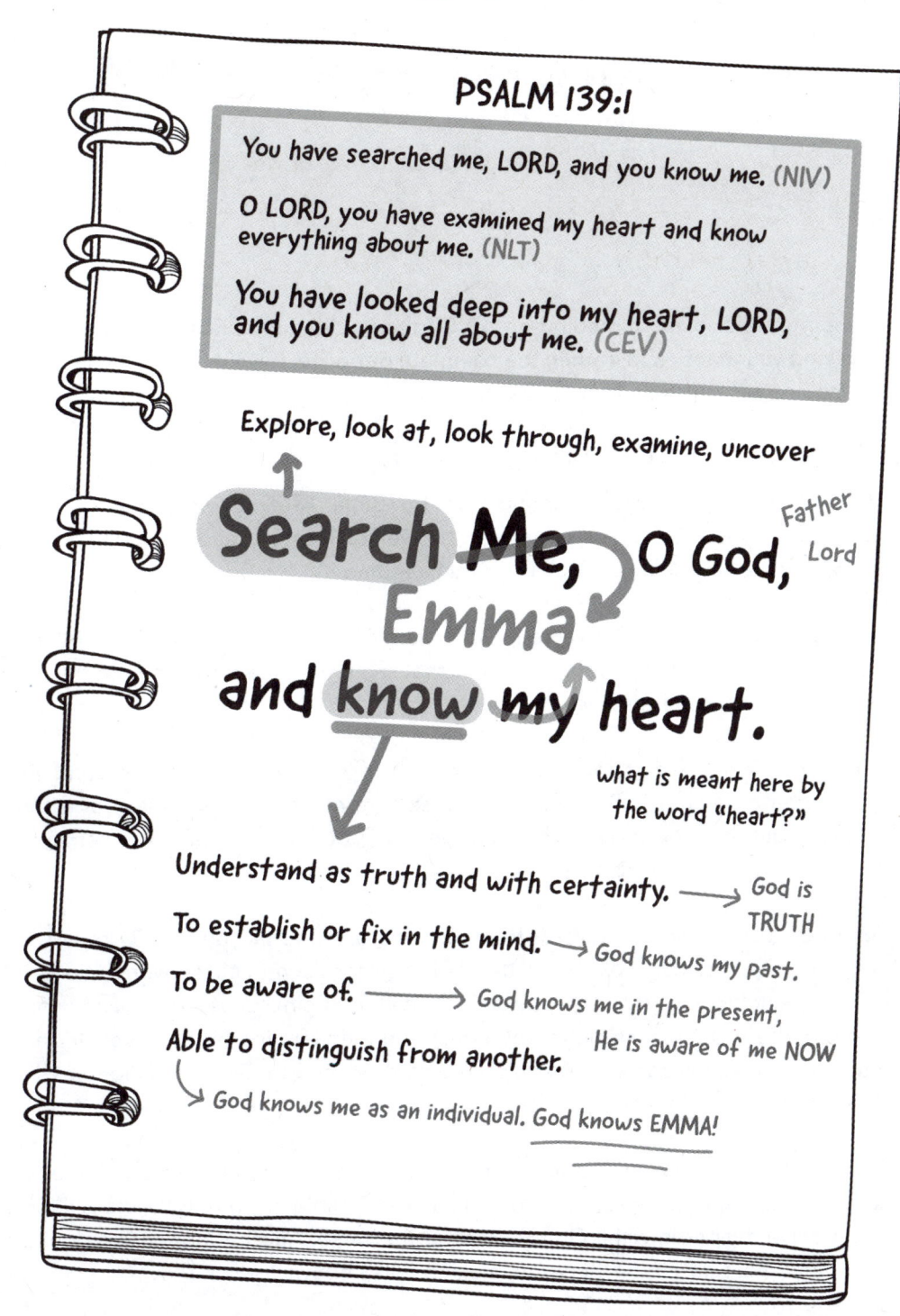

PSALM 139:1

You have searched me, LORD, and you know me. (NIV)

O LORD, you have examined my heart and know everything about me. (NLT)

You have looked deep into my heart, LORD, and you know all about me. (CEV)

Explore, look at, look through, examine, uncover

Search Me, O God, Emma and know my heart.

Father / Lord

what is meant here by the word "heart?"

Understand as truth and with certainty. → God is TRUTH

To establish or fix in the mind. → God knows my past.

To be aware of. → God knows me in the present, He is aware of me NOW

Able to distinguish from another.
↳ God knows me as an individual. God knows EMMA!

ENGAGING WITH SCRIPTURE — Soul Nourishment Resources

24. Simple Bible Meditation for Complete Beginners

"Our age has been sadly deficient in what may be termed spiritual greatness. At the root of this is the modern disease of shallowness. We are all too impatient to meditate on the faith we profess.... It is unhurried meditation on gospel truths and the exposing of our minds to these truths that yields the fruit of sanctified character."[37]

Maurice Roberts

The spiritual discipline of meditation is NOT the meditation of Eastern Mysticism, one of emptying your mind. It IS, rather, the complete opposite. It is the filling of your mind with a verse or passage and letting it soak in deeply.

Bible Meditation—One Method

READ. After praying, read a chapter from the Bible. After reading, locate a verse that stands out to you. Underline or notate that verse. Then re-read the verse a few more times, emphasizing different words on each reading.

WRITE. Next, write out the verse in your journal not as it appears in your Bible but in outline form. Separate the verse into lines that seem to make sense and put the different main points on a different line.

CONTEXT. Third, read and write down the context in which the verse was found. Re-read the chapter or section surrounding the verse to try to fully grasp what the author was talking about. Be very careful not to pull verses out of context, warping them into what you think they say or want them to say.

DEFINE. Now choose some words from the verse (even some you already know well) and pull out your dictionary. Write out the definition for each of these words. Some of the words in your Bible may already be notated with the original Greek words and definitions. If so, use those when possible to get a deeper understanding of the Greek. It's amazing how many Greek words have no equivalent words in English. Their language was so much richer than ours and these definitions really help.

STUDY. There are many possibilities here. You might use a commentary to look up any confusing passages or read the study notes in your Bible or other Bible translations. You might delve deeper into the Greek words of the verse. Another option is to look up the cross references noted for the verse, making notes on what you discover.

QUESTION. Next, ask questions. How does this apply to me? What is it telling me about God? About me? About Jesus? About how to live? Write down your thoughts to each question you ask.

QUOTES. There are some amazing theologians out there and their insights can be helpful. Use tools such as Blue Letter Bible or Bible Study Tools to search for these theologians and their insights, or search the Internet. While the technological advancements of our "day" are often blamed for our attention deficit and shallowness, they also make this "day" one of the best ages to study with great minds as we are able to sit under the teaching of these minds with just the click of a mouse.

WORSHIP. After working through the above steps (either all at once, or over the course of two or more days), you should find that you are naturally led into worship. Putting it all down on paper and organizing your thoughts about what God has done should lead you to fall down in worship, which naturally leads to prayer. Your time of prayer should most often mirror your worship. This is a time to thank God for what He has done and ask Him to help you in areas that the verse has spotlighted.[38]

> What value is there to reading one, three, or more chapters of Scripture only to find that after you've finished you can't recall a thing you've read?"[39]
>
> Donald Whitney

25. How to Meditate on God's Word

A few ideas:

- Read, read, and reread.

- Read it out loud.

- Read it several times, putting the emphasis on a different word each time.

- Read with a friend.

- Read with a pen (or a set of color pencils) – personalize, highlight, color code, circle, draw lines.

- Mark the different parts of speech.

- Make lists—characteristics, commands, promises, insights, etc.

- Find connections.

- Verse Map.

- Write it out by hand.

- Rewrite a verse or passage in your own words.

- Summarize it.

- Do a word study.

- Look for Christ. How does the passage point to Him?

- Ask, "What does this passage teach me about God?"

- Pray the Scriptures.

26. Biblical Reasons to Memorize Scripture

1. Jesus modeled it.
Then Jesus said to him, "Be gone, Satan! For it is written, 'You shall worship the Lord your God and him only shall you serve'"(Matthew 4:10).

2. It's a command.
Let the word of Christ dwell in you richly, teaching and admonishing one another in all wisdom, singing psalms and hymns and spiritual songs, with thankfulness in your hearts to God (Colossians 3:16).

3. To be formed into the image of Christ.
And we all, with unveiled face, beholding the glory of the Lord, are being transformed into the same image from one degree of glory to another. For this comes from the Lord who is the Spirit (2 Corinthians 3:18).

4. For the renewing of the mind and transforming of the life.
Do not be conformed to this world, but be transformed by the renewal of your mind, that by testing you may discern what is the will of God, what is good and acceptable and perfect (Romans 12:2).

5. To guard against sin.
I have stored up your word in my heart, that I might not sin against you (Psalm 119:11).

6. It helps us live in obedience.
But whoever looks intently into the perfect law that gives freedom, and continues in it—not forgetting what they have heard, but doing it—they will be blessed in what they do (James 1:25, NIV).

7. It helps us to better know God and his will.
But grow in the grace and knowledge of our Lord and Savior Jesus Christ. To him be the glory both now and to the day of eternity. Amen (2 Peter 3:18).

8. It leads to wisdom.
I understand more than the aged (Psalm 119:100).

9. It allows us to give counsel and comfort to other believers in Christ.
For whatever was written in former days was written for our instruction, that through endurance and through the encouragement of the Scriptures we might have hope (Romans 15:4).

10. It allows us to share the gospel with unbelievers.
But in your hearts honor Christ the Lord as holy, always being prepared to make a defense to anyone who asks you for a reason for the hope that is in you; yet do it with gentleness and respect (1 Peter 3:15).

11. It brings blessing to our lives
This Book of the Law shall not depart from your mouth, but you shall meditate on it day and night, so that you may be careful to do according to all that is written in it. For then you will make your way prosperous, and then you will have good success (Joshua 1:8).

12. Memorizing scripture is a means of communion with God.
But his delight is in the law of the Lord, and on his law he meditates day and night (Psalm 1:2).

The Lord is merciful and gracious, slow to anger and abounding in steadfast love. He will not always chide, nor will he keep his anger forever. He does not deal with us according to our sins, nor repay us according to our iniquities. For as high as the heavens are above the earth, so great is his steadfast love toward those who fear him; as far as the east is from the west, so far does he remove our transgressions from us. As a father shows compassion to his children, so the Lord shows compassion to those who fear him. For he knows our frame; he remembers that we are dust (Psalm 103:8–14).

> I know of no other single practice in the Christian life more rewarding, practically speaking, than memorizing Scripture. No other single exercise pays greater spiritual dividends! Your prayer life will be strengthened. Your witnessing will be sharper and much more effective. Your attitudes and outlook will begin to change. Your mind will become alert and observant. Your confidence and assurance will be enhanced. Your faith will be solidified.[40]
>
> Chuck Swindoll

27. Tips for Memorizing Scripture

- Write out by hand the Scripture you want to memorize. The physical act of writing is good for your brain and aids in retention.
- Say it out loud. Not just several times in one day, but over several days. The key is repetition over time.
- Review, review, review…and review some more! Begin each day's memorization session by reviewing previously memorized passages.
- Meditate on your Scripture. Word by word. Soak it in!
- Pray it.
- Sing it.
  - Make up your own song for a Scripture.
  - Locate a worship song that is based on the Scripture you are committing to memory.
  - Take the tune of a song you love and replace the words with Scripture.
  - Accompany yourself on a musical instrument as you sing.
- Photograph it. With your mind. Or literally. Take a picture of your Scripture and post it in a visible spot. BONUS IDEA: Make the passage your screen saver!
- Have your Bible nearby each time you review. When you just can't remember, take a look. It doesn't hurt. In fact, it will probably help in the long run.
- Memorize the verse numbers. When memorizing longer passages, include the verse number as if it were part of your verse. This practice will help you keep from dropping verses or phrases as you recite passages. It will also help you identify and pull out individual verses.
- Add feeling and interpretation as you recite your verses. This is actually a form of meditation and helps with internalization and recall.
- Ask a friend to listen as you recite a verse you are working on.

"Bible memorization is absolutely fundamental to spiritual formation. If I had to choose between all the disciplines of the spiritual life, I would choose Bible memorization, because it is a fundamental way of filling our minds with what it needs. This book of the law shall not depart out of your mouth. That's where you need it! How does it get in your mouth? Memorization."[41]

Dallas Willard

28. Scripture Memorization

All Scripture is breathed out by God and profitable for teaching, for reproof, for correction, and for training in righteousness.

2 Timothy 3:16

| **LONGER PASSAGES** VS. **SHORTER PASSAGES** | |
Chapters/Books	Single verses/2–3 consecutive verses
Follows the expository method of teaching and preaching.	Preference is given to "favorite" verses.
Scripture is considered in context.	Surrounding verses are not included.
Interact with verses we have never seen.	There is risk of missing out on something God has to say.
There is a flow.	Selection of memory work is often haphazard.
Lends itself to the discovery of new insights.	More apt to take things out of context.
Aids in understanding.	
Provides the opportunity to experience what God wanted to say through a particular author.	
Requires more time and effort to memorize.	Quicker and easier to memorize.

29. A Method for Memorizing Longer Scripture Passages

First Day:
Read the first verse of your chosen passage out loud ten times. Read it word-for-word. Look at each word on the page as you read.

After you have read the verse ten times, recite it ten times. Close your Bible or exit your app and say the verse ten times without looking.

Second Day:
Recite the previous day's verse ten times. If you need to, refresh your memory first by opening your Bible and reading the verse.

Now, move to the next verse. Just as you did on Day One, read it carefully, word-for-word, out loud ten times. When finished, cover the verse and recite it ten times.

Third Day:
Recite the previous day's verse ten times. Refresh your memory first if needed.

Next, recite the verses from all previous days together, verse one followed by verse two. Do this at least once. In the early days when the groupings of verses are short, it's a good idea to repeat this step multiple times.

Add the new verse. Read it out loud ten times. See each word as you read. Without looking, recite the verse ten times.

You're done for the day.

Continue with this same pattern until you have memorized an entire chapter or book of the Bible.

Pattern—Day One
Read the day's verse ten times, out loud, giving attention to each word as you read.

Without looking, recite the verse ten times.

Pattern—All Other Days:
Recite the previous day's verse ten times. Refresh your memory first if needed.

As a whole, recite all previous verses from the passage.

Read the day's new verse ten times, out loud, giving attention to each word as it is read.

Without looking, recite the verse ten times.

30. A Method for Memorizing Verses

Step One:
Read, read, read. Read your verse in context. Read the surrounding Scripture text. Read the verse in other translations. Read paraphrases of the verse. Read what others have written about the verse.

Step Two:
Read the verse itself several times. Read it out loud. Pay attention to each word on the page as you read.

Step Three:
Close your Bible and recite the verse eight to ten times.

Step Four:
The next day, open your Bible and read the verse again to refresh your memory. Close your Bible and recite the verse eight to ten times. Repeat this step daily until you feel you have the verse memorized.

Step Five:
With the verse committed to memory, choose a new verse and begin the process again.

Review:
As you work to memorize new verses, don't forget to REVIEW the old ones. Repeat newly memorized Scriptures often, daily, over many days.

31. Longer Passages for Scripture Memorization

Want to memorize longer passages of Scripture but don't know where to begin? Consider starting with one of the passages listed below.

- Genesis 1
- Psalm 1, 23, 46, 63, 100, 139, 150
- Matthew 5:1–12; 6:9–13
- John 1
- Romans 3, 8, 12
- 1 Corinthians 13
- 2 Corinthians 4
- Galatians 6
- Ephesians 4, 6
- The Book of Ephesians
- Philippians 2, 3
- Hebrews 12
- James 1
- 1 Peter 1
- 1 John 1
- 1 John 4
- The Book of 1 John

32. Fifty Important Scriptures to Memorize

- Numbers 13:30
- Deuteronomy 2:24
- Deuteronomy 30:11–14
- Joshua 1:3
- Joshua 17:17–18
- 2 Chronicles 16:9a
- Psalm 1:1-3
- Psalm 19:7–8
- Psalm 19:9–11
- Psalm 90:14
- Proverbs 3:5-6
- Proverbs 24:16
- Isaiah 26:3
- Isaiah 41:10
- Jeremiah 29:11
- Lamentations 3:22–23

- Ezekiel 36:26
- Zechariah 4:10
- Romans 5:8
- Romans 8:1
- Romans 8:6
- Romans 12:1–2
- 1 Corinthians 10:13
- 2 Corinthians 2:14
- 2 Corinthians 3:4–5
- 2 Corinthians 4:7
- 2 Corinthians 5:17
- 2 Corinthians 6:2
- 2 Corinthians 9:8
- 2 Corinthians 10:4–5
- 2 Corinthians 12:9
- Galatians 2:20

- Ephesians 1:3
- Ephesians 1:18–19
- Ephesians 2:12–13
- Ephesians 3:17–19
- Ephesians 3:20
- Ephesians 6:10
- Philippians 2:13
- Philippians 4:8
- Philippians 4:13
- Colossians 1:21–22
- Colossians 2:10
- Colossians 3:1–3
- 1 Thessalonians 5:18
- 2 Timothy 1:7
- Titus 2:11–12
- Hebrews 2:1–3a
- 2 Peter 1:3
- 1 John 4:8[42]

33. "Soul" Verses (A Partial List)

Deuteronomy 6:5
You shall love the LORD your God with all your heart and with all your soul and with all your might.

Psalm 19:7
The law of the LORD is perfect, reviving the soul; the testimony of the LORD is sure, making wise the simple.

Psalm 42:11
Why are you cast down, O my soul, and why are you in turmoil within me? Hope in God; for I shall again praise him, my salvation and my God.

Psalm 84:2
My soul longs, yes, faints for the courts of the LORD; my heart and flesh sing for joy to the living God.

Psalm 103:1
Bless the LORD, O my soul, and all that is within me, bless his holy name!

Psalm 131:1–2
O LORD, my heart is not lifted up; my eyes are not raised too high; I do not occupy myself with things too great and too marvelous for me. But I have calmed and quieted my soul, like a weaned child with its mother; like a weaned child is my soul within me.

Psalm 139:14
I praise you, for I am fearfully and wonderfully made. Wonderful are your works; my soul knows it very well.

Jeremiah 6:16
Thus says the LORD: "Stand by the roads, and look, and ask for the ancient paths, where the good way is; and walk in it, and find rest for your souls."

Matthew 10:28
And do not fear those who kill the body but cannot kill the soul. Rather fear him who can destroy both soul and body in hell.

Matthew 22:37–38
And he said to him, "You shall love the Lord your God with all your heart and with all your soul and with all your mind. This is the great and first commandment."

34. Soul Nourishment Scriptures (A Partial List)

(*Italics* – emphasis on soul nourishment terms.)

Psalm 51:10
Create in me a clean heart, O God, and renew a right spirit within me.

Psalm 1:1–5
Blessed is the man who walks not in the counsel of the wicked, nor stands in the way of sinners, nor sits in the seat of scoffers; but his *delight is in the law of the* Lord, *and on his law he meditates day and night*. He is like a tree planted by streams of water that yields its fruit in its season, and its leaf does not wither. In all that he does, he prospers. The wicked are not so, but are like chaff that the wind drives away. Therefore the wicked will not stand in the judgment, nor sinners in the congregation of the righteous.

Isaiah 55:1–3
Come, everyone who thirsts, come to the waters; and he who has no money, come, buy and eat! Come, buy wine and milk without money and without price. Why do you spend your money for that which is not bread, and your labor for that which does not satisfy? *Listen* diligently to me, and *eat* what is good, and *delight* yourselves in rich food. *Incline* your ear, and *come* to me; hear, that your soul may live; and I will make with you an everlasting covenant, my steadfast, sure love for David."

Isaiah 55:6
"*Seek* the Lord while he may be found; *call* upon him while he is near."

John 4:3–6
[H]e left Judea and departed again for Galilee. And he had to pass through Samaria. So he came to a town of Samaria called Sychar, near the field that Jacob had given to his son Joseph. Jacob's well was there; so Jesus, *wearied* as he was from his journey, *was sitting beside the well*. It was about the sixth hour.

John 6:31–40
"Our fathers ate the manna in the wilderness; as it is written, 'He gave them bread from heaven to eat.'" Jesus then said to them, "Truly, truly, I say to you, it was not Moses who gave you the bread from heaven, but my Father gives you the true bread from heaven. For the bread of God is he who comes down from heaven and gives life to the world." They said to him, "Sir, give us this bread always." Jesus said to them, "I am the bread of life; *whoever comes to me* shall not hunger, and *whoever believes* in me shall never thirst. But I said to you that you have seen me and yet do not believe. All that the Father gives me will come to me, and whoever comes to me I will never cast out. For I have come down

from heaven, not to do my own will but the will of him who sent me. And this is the will of him who sent me, that I should lose nothing of all that he has given me, but raise it up on the last day. For this is the will of my Father, that everyone who looks on the Son and believes in him should have eternal life, and I will raise him up on the last day."

John 15:4–5
Abide in me, and I in you. As the branch cannot bear fruit by itself, unless it abides in the vine, neither can you, unless you abide in me. I am the vine; you are the branches. Whoever abides in me and I in him, he it is that bears much fruit, for apart from me you can do nothing.

Romans 10:17
So faith comes from *hearing*, and hearing through the word of Christ.

Hebrews 2:1–3
Therefore we must *pay much closer attention* to what we have heard, lest we drift away from it. For since the message declared by angels proved to be reliable, and every transgression or disobedience received a just retribution, how shall we escape if we neglect such a great salvation? It was declared at first by the Lord, and it was attested to us by those who heard,

1 Peter 1:22–25
Having purified your souls by your *obedience to the truth* for a sincere brotherly love, *love* one another earnestly from a pure heart, since you have been born again, not of perishable seed but of imperishable, through the living and abiding word of God; for "All flesh is like grass and all its glory like the flower of grass. The grass withers, and the flower falls, but the word of the Lord remains forever." And this word is the good news that was preached to you.

1 Peter 2:1–2
So put away all malice and all deceit and hypocrisy and envy and all slander. Like newborn infants, *long* for the pure spiritual milk, that by it you may grow up into salvation.

Solitude & Silence

SOUL NOURISHMENT RESOURCES

35. Tips for Enjoying a Time of Solitude

And he said to them,

"Come away by yourselves to a desolate place and rest a while."

Mark 6:31

SOLITUDE is perhaps one of the most difficult spiritual disciplines for us to implement. And for so many reasons: no time, too busy, can't be still that long, driven mad by the quiet, or we simply don't know how to go about this thing called SOLITUDE.

Don't let the excuses win out, use this list as a starting point. Then begin to weave this precious discipline into your life rhythm.

1. Prepare

- Plan it. Put your time of solitude on your calendar. Rearrange schedules if necessary.

- Choose a place. Base your selection on the amount of time available to you. If you only have a few hours, prepare a spot in your home or head out to a nearby park or local coffee shop. You might even choose to observe the time in your church sanctuary if it is available. (If you have small children, arrange for a babysitter or call Grandma!) For those times when you have a couple of days or so to devote to your time of solitude, consider scheduling a visit to a retreat center, hotel, cabin in the woods, or your favorite beach.

- Pack a bag. Think ahead about what you need to take along and make sure you have it with you. (Again, this will depend on the amount of time you have for this experience.) Items to consider: Your Bible, an alternate translation (for hearing the words from a fresh perspective), a journal, something to write with, water, snacks, additional clothing and toiletries for over-nights. These items are important. You don't want your time interrupted because you have to go get something; however, take care not to place too much emphasis on the "things." This time away is all about spending uninterrupted time with God.

2. Enter

Begin your time with no agenda. That's a hard one for many of us, myself included. If it's hard for you, then acknowledge it. Begin by giving your agenda to God. Agenda or not, surrender this time of solitude to Him.

3. Sit in Silence

Take the first twenty or thirty minutes to do nothing except listen. (Of course, this time frame can be adjusted based on the total amount of time you have allotted to your particular solitude experience.) During this time simply be quiet. Don't speak. I know, this one is difficult. We want to talk. Our default is to talk. But fight through it. Be quiet. Simply sit in the stillness. Or be quiet as you take a lingering stroll. Be a listener, not a speaker.

4. Give Thanks

Gratitude is evidence of not being in a hurry. A hurried life often fails to see. It fails to pause. As a result, the giving of thanks is seldom offered. Time is required for one to notice and acknowledge.

5. Linger

Become as quiet on the outside as you are able. Linger with your Heavenly Father. We are doers. We want to make the most of our time and are, therefore, so often tempted to be DOING good things (and as many as possible, at that). This time of solitude is a time to be alone and quiet in His welcoming presence. Choose to simply be. Be present. Be attentive. He is enjoying your presence. Enjoy His.

6. Sola Scriptura

The Bible is God's very word. Remember: during times of solitude we want to resist "doing." Reading God's Word, however, is a wonderful way to sit with Him and enjoy His presence.

7. Get a Handle on Distractions

When distractions come, and they WILL come, choose to let them pass on by. If that strategy doesn't work for you, try keeping a pad of paper and pen nearby so you can jot them down as they come to mind and then move on. Another option is to make the choice to include your distractions in your time with the Lord: give thanks to Him for them, make a request concerning them, or commit them to His care.

8. Bring Closure

Just as you made intentional preparation for this time of solitude, be sure to be intentional in bringing it to a close: reflect, give thanks, journal, pray. Create your own "closing tradition."

Weave these times of solitude into your life rhythm as often as you need (as often as it takes for your soul to receive nourishment and to be healthy). Your schedule may allow weekly observances, or it may require monthly, bi-monthly, or quarterly observances. Rhythm and variation may even be found in your SOLITUDE schedule as you choose to plan monthly two-hour times of solitude with a once or twice a year two-day observance.

36. Extended Personal Communion with God (EPC)

"Come away by yourselves to a desolate place and rest a while."

Mark 6:31

The purpose of Extended Personal Communion with God (EPC) is simply to "be" with Him. For at least a few hours once a month or so, schedule time away to be alone and quiet in God's welcoming presence.

Tips for EPC

Relinquish Agendas
"Being" is so much more difficult than "doing." Periods of EPC provide opportunity for "being," that is time and space for attentiveness and responsiveness to God. Enter EPC with a clear mind, ready to listen. On those occasions when it is simply not possible to leave your agenda behind, begin your time of EPC by acknowledging whatever you have brought to this time.

Listen
Devote the first twenty to thirty minutes of your EPC to listening. Find a quiet hideaway or go for a solitary walk. Enter the presence of the Lord, prayerfully, as a listener rather than a speaker.

Offer Thanks
Thanksgiving slows us and turns our focus toward Jesus. Notice the good. Say thank you.

Intentionally Quiet Yourself
Become as quiet on the outside as you are able. Be still and silent in God's presence. When thoughts of "doing" come (and they will), choose to linger.

Have a Distraction Plan
Just as thoughts of "doing" will arise, so will distractions. Be prepared. Have a plan. Consider having a note pad and pen nearby. As distractions enter your mind, jot them down and let them go. Another idea is to acknowledge the distractions in prayer before the Lord as soon as they arise.[43]

37. Ways to Nourish Your Soul through Solitude and Silence

1. In the stillness of the morning, spend 10–15 quiet minutes engaging with God in His Scriptures or in prayer.

2. Set a timer for 5 minutes. Find a quiet spot away from the noise and simply sit with God.

3. Make solitude and silence part of your daily habit. Connect this time to something you already do. Enjoy your time of solitude with your morning cup of coffee. Linger for 5–10 minutes after lunch. Take a daily solitude walk or experience some silence while sitting on the patio at the end of the day.

4. Go for a leisurely walk, no phone, no earbuds. Talk with God as you walk or simply stroll in silence.

5. Cozy up in a quiet little corner of your nearby coffee shop. Take your Bible or journal and spend an hour or so in reading, study, or reflection.

6. Once a month or at some regular interval, schedule someone to watch your children. Use the time for some silence and solitude with your Heavenly Father.

7. Grab your lawn chair and spend a few hours sitting under the shade trees or by the pond of a nearby park.

8. Enjoy an extended retreat. Make arrangements to get away for an entire day or weekend. Choose a location that is personally inviting and relaxing.

Soul Searching

SOUL NOURISHMENT RESOURCES

38. Questions for Searching the Soul

- Am I hearing from God?
- Have I lost my joy?
- Am I producing spiritual fruit?
- Am I experiencing victory in my life?
- Have I grown in the last five years? In the last year?
- Do I love God more today than I did before?
- How well am I obeying His Word?
- What are the priorities in my life?
- In what areas of my life am I still not putting God first?
- What in my past is interfering with me doing God's will?
- Do I always try to have an "attitude of gratitude" or do I find myself always complaining about my circumstances?
- In what areas of my life am I ungrateful?
- Have I gotten angry and easily blown up at people?
- Have I been sarcastic?
- What in my past is still causing me fear or anxiety?
- In what past dealing was I dishonest?
- Have I exaggerated who I am to make myself look better?
- In what areas of my past have I used false humility?
- Have I pretended to live one way in front of my Christian friends and another way at home or at work?
- Am I investing my life into the lives of others?

39. Questions for Reflecting on Your Life's Direction

1. What's one thing you could do this year to increase your enjoyment of God?
2. What's the most humanly impossible thing you will ask God to do this year?
3. What's the single most important thing you could do to improve the quality of your family life this year?
4. In which spiritual discipline do you most want to make progress this year, and what will you do about it?
5. What is the single biggest time-waster in your life, and what will you do about it this year?
6. What is the most helpful new way you could strengthen your church?
7. For whose salvation will you pray most fervently this year?
8. What's the most important way you will, by God's grace, try to make this year different from last year?
9. What one thing could you do to improve your prayer life this year?
10. What single thing that you plan to do this year will matter most in ten years? In eternity?

In addition to these ten questions, here are twenty-one more to help you "Consider your ways." Think on the entire list at one sitting or answer one question each day for a month.

11. What's the most important decision you need to make this year?
12. What area of your life most needs simplifying, and what's one way you could simplify in that area?
13. What's the most important need you feel burdened to meet this year?
14. What habit would you most like to establish this year?
15. Who is the person you most want to encourage this year?
16. What is your most important financial goal this year, and what is the most important step you can take toward achieving it?

17. What's the single most important thing you could do to improve the quality of your work life this year?

18. What's one new way you could be a blessing to your pastor (or to another who ministers to you) this year?

19. What's one thing you could do this year to enrich the spiritual legacy you will leave to your children and grandchildren?

20. What book, in addition to the Bible, do you most want to read this year?

21. What one thing do you most regret about last year, and what will you do about it this year?

22. What single blessing from God do you want to seek most earnestly this year?

23. In what area of your life do you most need growth, and what will you do about it this year?

24. What's the most important trip you want to take this year?

25. What skill do you most want to learn or improve this year?

26. To what need or ministry will you try to give an unprecedented amount this year?

27. What's the single most important thing you could do to improve the quality of your commute this year?

28. What one biblical doctrine do you most want to understand better this year, and what will you do about it?

29. If those who know you best gave you one piece of advice, what would they say? Would they be right? What will you do about it?

30. What's the most important new item you want to buy this year?

31. In what area of your life do you most need change, and what will you do about it this year?[44]

40. Self-Reflection Questions by Category

My personal relationship with Christ

- Has there ever been a time in my life that I was more in love with God than I am right now?
- Am I listening to the Word and choosing it in every area of my life?
- Am I worshipping Him for who He is, not for what He does for me?
- Am I honoring Jesus as King?
- Am I following the Holy Spirit?
- Am I modeling His nature and character in my choices and taking every thought captive and making it obedient to Christ?
- Am I spending time with Him?
- Is the gospel making a difference in my life?
- What have I been learning about God recently?

My attitude

- Do I have the heart of a servant?
- Am I serving from pure motives?
- Have I made others look good this week?
- Have I made someone's life a bit easier this week?
- Am I a team player?
- What is my attitude toward family members?
- What is my attitude toward others in general?
- Am I grumbling and complaining?
- How am I showing gratitude?
- Am I enjoying the trip?
- Do I have a heart after God?
- Am I making it all about me?

My priorities

- Am I able to list the top ten priorities for my life right this very moment?
- Are these priorities in line with the Bible?
- Do my actions and decisions correspond with my listed priorities?
- What would my family members or close friends say are my top five priorities?
- Do I need to realign my priorities?

My time management

- How am I spending my time?
- Am I spending time daily with the Lord?
- Am I allowing time to rule my day? My life?
- Is my family suffering because of my misuse of time?
- Am I making space for relationships?
- Am I making time for my personal growth and development?
- Am I identifying the time robbers in my life?

My performance

- Am I a team player?
- Am I seeking my own glory?
- Have I invested in others?
- How have I encouraged someone recently?
- What am I doing that someone else can do?
- Am I a clear and skillful communicator?
- Am I skilled at solving problems?
- Can I be relied on to complete assignments and keep commitments?
- If I had to rate my performance level on a scale of 1 to 10, what would it be?
- Am I meeting the needs of those who depend on me?

In each area

- What am I currently doing that I need to say **no** to?
- Is there a better way to do it?
- Am I truly listening?

41. A Daily Personal Audit

- At the end of your day, pull away to a solitary place.
- Quiet your heart and mind.
- Pray. Invite the Holy Spirit into this time and ask Him to guide your thoughts.
- Close your eyes. Review the day's events in your mind. Watch the day play out as a movie on the back of your eyelids.
- Pay attention.
    - Watch for the "highlights"—moments when God felt near.
    - Watch for the "retakes"—moments you would like to do over.
    - Respond to the "highlights" and the "retakes."
    - Thank God for the moments of your day that made the "highlight" reel.
    - Seek forgiveness where the "retakes" indicate it is needed.
- Rest a few moments in God's love for you.

The steadfast love of the Lord never ceases; his mercies never come to an end; they are new every morning; great is your faithfulness.

Lamentations 3:22–23

Soul Friendship

SOUL NOURISHMENT RESOURCES

42. Cultivating a Soul Friendship

A soul friendship will not just happen on its own accord. For many people, it begins with an intense search.

What are we looking for?

Energy: Do you come away from time with certain friends feeling more energized than you do after you have spent time with others? Who are the people in your life that give you energy? Who is it that leaves you with a greater sense of spiritual vitality? In other words, who in your life is "life-giving?"

Matching: After identifying someone in your life who has that intangible energizing factor, you will want to begin the process of exploring the possibility of deepening the relationship. One indicator to pay attention to is the idea of "matching" intimacy levels. This means you are "matching" the vulnerability level of the friendship. As you open up deeper and deeper areas of your soul, your friend should reciprocate. The withholding of intimacy is a sign that a relationship is not moving toward becoming a soul friendship at this point in time. The sooner you realize and adjust your expectations, the better. If they listen intently but never "match" your vulnerability level, you would do well to look elsewhere for your soul friend.

Confidentiality: In searching out a soul friend, you must take into consideration a prospective friend's capacity to hold a confidence. This is such a serious matter that you might even consider administering a "confidentiality test." Such a test involves sharing something more personal in nature with a prospective soul friend (but nothing personal enough that it would put you at risk if the test fails). After sharing, wait a couple of weeks and then check in. Ask your prospective soul friend point-blank if they have shared the information with anyone. If not, tell them what you were doing and why. It is important to realize that many people may want to be your "friend" for a variety of reasons, not all of which may be good. In addition to that, there are well-meaning people who simply cannot keep a secret. They are not bad people; they just cannot keep a secret. You need to know this ahead of time before you have entrusted something to them unwisely. Believe the best in others but be wise.[45]

43. A Soul Friend is...

A Good Listener
Actively listen. Lean in. Truly being heard makes a person feel special.

A Judgment-Free Zone
Offer grace, not judgment. In the freedom of authenticity and vulnerability an atmosphere of normalcy and safety grows. Spiritual growth is also encouraged in a judgment-free zone.

Appreciative
Communicate appreciation. Don't just think it. Do something to show it. Send texts letting your friend know you are thinking of her, meet for coffee to ask for updates on her life, mail a card on important holidays or for absolutely no reason at all.

Loyal
Practice loyalty. Make "I've got your back" come to life. Do not share your friend's confidences with others or talk behind your friend's back. Stand up for her if or when others demonstrate disloyalty.

An Effective Communicator
Communicate clearly and effectively. Express your feelings, address issues head-on, apologize when you are in the wrong. Do not get into the habit of sweeping things under the rug.

Honest
Honesty is the best policy even though it can be hard at times. A soul friend has the responsibility of speaking truth into her friend's life.

An Initiator
Initiate. Don't wait for your friend to ask. Soul friendships cannot be one-sided. Text to arrange that coffee date, call to see how the job interview or doctor's appointment went, make plans for a girls' night out. Put forth the effort.

In It for the Long Haul
Enjoy the good times of your friendship, but more importantly, be there for your friend to lean on through the bad.

Dependable
Follow through. If you say you are going to do something, do it even when you don't feel like it, even when something better comes along.

Vulnerable
Open up. Share things. Hard things. In order for a friendship to grow, both parties need to be vulnerable. Increased trust within a friendship will deepen the connection.

44. Simple Ways to Show You Care

Always be looking for opportunities to reach out and bless someone else. Ask questions and take time to really listen to the responses. Be a giver. Pour into others.

- When you are waiting in line at the grocery store, text your friend to let her know you are thinking of her or to just check in and see how she is doing.
- When you are waiting in the carpool pick-up line, jot a quick note to a friend who is going through a rough patch and mail it.
- When you are working on laundry or cleaning, call your friend.
- If you have a free evening or weekend, invite your friend to join you for dinner, a game, or a movie.
- If you see a great deal on an item friends you know love, shoot a quick text to let them know. Or better yet, buy it for them and surprise them with it "just because."
- Create a hand-made card and write a thoughtful note.
- Randomly, without any prompting, look your friend in the eye and say, "I really appreciate you—just for being you."
- Compliment a friend on something people may not often acknowledge, like work ethic or consideration for other people.
- Send a funny video from YouTube and write, "You make me laugh more than this video. Thank you!"
- Give her something of yours that reminds you of her.
- Give a book you have already read inscribed with a meaningful message.
- Ask if you can take care of some responsibilities; for example, you could offer to pick up your friend's children from school.
- Tell her she was so right about something and let her know how that information impacted your life.
- Squeeze your friend's hand and say, "Thank you."
- Ask, "How are you—really?" Then do nothing but listen and respond to what you hear for as long as your friend needs to talk.
- Ask, "What can I do to help you today?"
- Notice how your friend affects other people—not you—and comment on it.
- Cook dinner for your friend.
- Make a simple sacrifice to spend time with her.

- See potential and encourage your friend to pursue her dreams.
- Ask for a retelling of her favorite story.
- Let your friend decide what the two of you will do and find a way to really enjoy it—go line dancing and see the experience through your friend's eyes.
- Offer your skill for free.
- Tell her which qualities of hers you admire.
- Introduce her to someone as, "My dear friend who taught me…"
- Introduce her to something new that you think would enrich her life.
- Let her be right, even if you think she's not, if it's not that big of a deal.
- Ask for advice on something important and share what the opinion means to you.
- Send a text that reads, "Thought of you today, and it made me smile."
- Notice when your friend does something that might have been challenging and applaud the efforts.
- Tell a friend the block in your planner that includes her name is the most important on a busy day.
- Tell her you understand her struggle—whatever that may be—and say you are always a call away to help.
- Say thank you for something she might not realize she gave you, like inspiration to seize the day or the courage to leave an unhealthy relationship.
- Let her know how she helped you think about something differently. For example, tell how your friend helped you see losing your job as a gift.
- Surprise her in some way with something you know she will enjoy.
- Send a picture of you together and remind her why that day was amazing.
- Share her pain. Hold her hand, wipe her tears, and be her shoulder to lean on.
- Give her an uncomfortably long hug.
- Share a childlike experience with your friend. Go on the swings, get some ice cream, and let go of your stresses together.
- Invite her out with friends of yours she does not know. Nothing says "I value you" like inclusion.
- Look out for her loved ones.
- Remember something she said that she thought you did not hear.
- Simply say, "I really care about you, and I wanted you to know."

45. How to Encourage

Encouragement:

- Encouragement is an essential skill of a biblically healthy community.

- Real encouragement is more about sightedness than it is about explanation.

- Encouragement is not just about making people feel and think better, it is about stimulating spiritual imagination.

- We need eyes to see this one amazing reality: We are Christ's, and He is ours.

Give each other eyes to see three things:

1. Christ's Presence

- Your goal here is to help people develop a "Christ is with me" mentality.

- This perspective on life is found in Psalm 46:1–2.

2. Christ's Promises

- I can encourage you by helping you remember what is promised.

- These are not pie-in-the-sky unrealities but an accurate assessment of our true resources as children of God.

3. Our Potential in Christ

- When we struggle, we measure our potential; however, most of us are poor personal accountants.

- When we add up the things that define our potential, we leave out the most important asset: our potential *is* Christ! (Galatians 2:20).

Looking at our situation through the lens of His presence and provision changes our view of things and helps us to encourage each other.[46]

46. Twenty Things to Say to Encourage a Friend

1. Me, too.
2. I understand.
3. Keep going. You can do it!
4. What a wonderful idea!
5. I would love to pray with you about it.
6. How did it go?
7. That is fantastic!
8. Thank you for being my friend.
9. Text me!
10. Let me know how it goes. I'll be praying.
11. Do you need to talk?
12. I really appreciate you!
13. Have a fantastic time!
14. You have worked hard; you deserve it!
15. Way to go. You did great!
16. Let's celebrate that accomplishment!
17. I was so impressed with the way you handled that.
18. You are a fabulous example in that area.
19. Is there anything I can do to help?
20. I brought you some chocolate. (*PS: Only say this if the chocolate actually accompanies the statement. Otherwise, you won't be considered a good friend. Or a friend at all.*)[47]

47. Soul-Building Words

- I'm thankful for you.
- You make my day better.
- You make my life better.
- I love spending time with you.
- Thank you.
- Seeing your face makes me happy.
- I love that we are friends.
- I'm listening.
- I can't wait to hear all about it.
- Let's do it your way.
- I care.
- This time is all yours.
- Me, too!
- I appreciate you.
- How can I be a better _____ (parent, friend, spouse) to you?
- What do you think?
- Nothing is more important than being with you right now.
- Yes, let's!
- How can I help?
- Take your time. You don't have to rush.
- I think you are doing a tremendous job.
- You are very good at that!
- Keep going. You've got this.
- I understand.
- That's a great question.
- Your effort was remarkable.
- That was brave.
- I believe in you.
- You were right.
- I trust you.
- I am amazed at how much you are handling right now.
- I am learning a lot from you by watching you do something so challenging.
- This isn't over—there's still time to turn this around.
- That was a good choice.
- I forgive you.
- You are not alone.
- I love you.

48. Ways to Bless Friends Going Through a Difficult Time

1. Ask, "What can I do for you this week?"
   - Don't let them off the hook. Make suggestions if they don't come up with something on their own. Examples: run errands, sit at their house while they run errands, or take them for coffee. Consider making multiple suggestions and having them choose one.
   - Once you have made the offer, commit yourself to following through. Do not bail.
2. Ask, "How can I pray for you?"
3. Pray.
   - Send a note, call, text, or email to let them know you are praying for them.
   - Pray with them when you visit.
   - Call and pray with them over the phone.
4. Drop them an email.
5. Do not forget the children. (This includes siblings of a child who may be going through a difficult time.)
   - Take children or siblings to lunch or for ice cream.
   - Get them out of the house. Go to a movie or the park.
   - Provide gift cards for a treat of some kind.
6. Take a crockpot meal to the family.
   - Just make double of what you are preparing for your own family.
7. Share your favorite praise music with the family.
8. Share a favorite speaker or preacher.
9. Give restaurant gift cards.
10. If the family does not live in your town, send gift cards or freezer meals.
11. Write out your favorite Bible verses on cards and give to the family.

12. If the situation involves a hospital stay, make a photo collage for the hospital room.
    - It brightens the room.
    - Collages help the healthcare providers make connections to the patient.
13. Buy a copy of a favorite book and give to the family.
14. Fill the family's home with groceries or household staples.
15. Mail cards with handwritten notes inside. There's nothing quite so encouraging as knowing someone cares enough to take the time to write a note.

49. The "One Anothers"

- **Love** one another (John 13:34–35; John 15:12; John 15:17; Romans 12:10; Romans 13:8; 1 Thessalonians 4:9; 1 Peter 1:22; 1 John 3:11; 1 John 3:23; 1 John 4:7; 1 John 4:11; 2 John 1:5).

- **Be at peace** with one another (Mark 9:50).

- **Outdo** one another in **showing honor** (Romans 12:10).

- **Live in harmony** with one another (Romans 12:16; Romans 15:5).

- **Welcome** one another (Romans 15:7).

- **Instruct** one another (Romans 15:14).

- **Care** for one another (1 Corinthians 12:25).

- **Serve** one another (Galatians 5:13).

- **Bear** one another's **burdens** (Galatians 6:2).

- **Bear** with one another (Ephesians 4:2).

- **Be kind** one to another (Ephesians 4:32).

- **Forgive** one another (Ephesians 4:32).

- **Speak** to one another **in psalms, hymns, and spiritual songs** (Ephesians 5:19).

- **Submit** to one another (Ephesians 5:21).

- **Bear** with one another (Colossians 3:13).

- **Forgive** one another (Colossians 3:13).

- **Teach** one another (Colossians 3:16).

- **Admonish** one another (Colossians 3:16).

- **Encourage** one another (1 Thessalonians 4:18; 1 Thessalonians 5:11)

- **Build** one another **up** (1 Thessalonians 5:11).

- **Exhort** one another (Hebrews 3:13).

- **Stir up** one another **to love and good works** (Hebrews 10:24).

- **Confess your sins** to one another (James 5:16).

- **Pray** for one another (James 5:16).

- **Show hospitality** to one another (1 Peter 4:9).

- **Serve** one another (1 Peter 4:10).

- **Clothe yourselves with humility** toward one another (1 Peter 5:5).

Simplicity

SOUL NOURISHMENT RESOURCES

50. Ways to Practice Surrender

I appeal to you therefore, brothers, by the mercies of God, to present your bodies as a living sacrifice, holy and acceptable to God, which is your spiritual worship. Do not be conformed to this world, but be transformed by the renewal of your mind, that by testing you may discern what is the will of God, what is good and acceptable and perfect.

Romans 12:1-2

Jesus' instruction regarding surrender:

Then Jesus told his disciples, "If anyone would come after me, let him deny himself and take up his cross and follow me. For whoever would save his life will lose it, but whoever loses his life for my sake will find it (Matthew 16:24–25).

Jesus' example of surrender:

And he said, "Abba, Father, all things are possible for you. Remove this cup from me. Yet not what I will, but what you will" (Mark 14:36).

- Pray a prayer of surrender each morning before your feet hit the floor.
- On your knees, before the day begins, surrender yourself and your day to God.
- Utter breath prayers throughout your day.
    - › "God, I surrender myself to you."
    - › "God, I offer myself to you."
    - › "God, I surrender _____ to you."
    - › "God, I give _____ to you."
- Surrender your need for control.
- Pray a meaningful passage of Scripture as a prayer of surrender to the Lord.
- Search on the internet for a prayer of surrender. Choose one that has special meaning to you and recite it daily or as desired.
- Write your own prayer of surrender.
- Write a letter of surrender to God.

- Abide.

    - Spend some time in your Sacred Space.
    - Be still with God.
    - Surrender your mind—WHAT and HOW you think.
    - Surrender your body.
    - Surrender your will.
    - Trust!
    - Give it to God. Pray, "God, You are Lord of _____."
    - Seek God.
    - Self-reflect. Ask:
        › "Am I totally surrendered to God?"
        › "How am I exhibiting a life of daily surrender?"
        › "What am I still holding on to?"
        › "What area(s) have I not surrendered to God?"
        › "What is keeping me from surrendering _____ to God?"
    - Ask a soul friend to hold you accountable.

51. Celebrating the Christian Year

The Cycle of Light
(Celebrating the Incarnation—God with us)

Advent (A Season of Waiting)—Wait
Advent is the beginning of the church year and begins on the fourth Sunday before Christmas Day. It originated as a period of fasting in preparation for the Feast of the Nativity (Christmas). Advent is about waiting for the coming of Christmas and for the second coming of Christ.

Those who observe Advent generally spend their time rethinking their priorities, realigning their lives with God's desires, seeking forgiveness, and beginning again.

Each of the four Sundays of Advent has a watchword:

- First Sunday—Wait
- Second Sunday—Prepare
- Third Sunday—Rejoice
- Fourth Sunda—Love

Christmas (A Season of Celebration)—Wonder
A celebration of the birth of the Word, the Light of the World, the Son of God. Within the context of the Christian calendar, Christmas is not confined to a single day. Rather, Christmas is a season of the church year. Its twelve days of feast spans from Christmas Day through January 6, Epiphany.

Epiphany (The Season of Light)
Epiphany begins on January 6 and runs through the Sunday immediately preceding Ash Wednesday. It is a season for celebrating the good news of the coming of Jesus for the whole earth. "Epiphany" comes from the Greek verb *phainein* which means "to cause to appear" or "to bring to light."

Three events in the life of Christ are associated with the Feast of the Epiphany:

- the visit of the wise men from the East
- the baptism of Jesus by John in the Jordan River
- the turning of water into wine at Cana

Epiphany is a season for seeing more of Christ's glory. Observers of Epiphany focus their eyes and heart on the life and mission of Jesus Christ. This is a season for abiding in the Story and sharing the Story with others.

The Cycle of Life
(Contemplating Salvation—God for us)

Lent (A Season of Darkness)
Much like Advent, Lent is a time of preparation. The season of Lent provides opportunity to reckon with the reality of darkness and death and life in a fallen world. It is a time to look inward and acknowledge our vulnerabilities and a time to look outward and weigh the costs of discipleship. Again, like Advent, Lent is a time to swing wide our heart's door and grow to understand our Lord a little deeper.

The Paschal Triduum
The word Triduum comes from the Latin word meaning "three days." Maundy Thursday, Good Friday, and Holy Saturday comprise the Paschal Triduum which begins at sundown on Thursday and ends at sundown on Sunday. It celebrates the death and resurrection of Jesus Christ, which is the heart of Christianity.

Easter (A Season of Joy)
Easter is the celebration of Christ's resurrection. Don't just gloss over that statement as we are so often prone to do. Stop and let that soak in a moment: Christ risen, death defeated, sins forgiven, evil overcome, no consequences.

Yes, Easter is a day, but how can we contain such magnitude in a single day? In the Christian calendar, Easter is a season, a season of celebration. During Easter's fifty days, we celebrate the event that rocked our world and changed everything.

The Cycle of Love
(Concentrating on the Outworking of Redemption—God through us)

Ordinary Time
At the culmination of the Easter season, Pentecost marks the beginning of Ordinary Time. Ordinary comes from the Latin root meaning "order." When something is ordered, it is arranged in sequence, numbered. It is ordinal. Ordinary Time, a lengthy six month season, is counted time. During Ordinary Time the Sundays are simply numbered.

While each of the other seasons of the Christian calendar has a singular focus, Sundays in Ordinary Time are devoted to all aspects of the mystery of Christ. This season is a time set aside for reflecting on and celebrating our call to follow Jesus daily by faithfully giving attention to our formation, devotion, ministry, and mission as the life of Christ is lived through us.

Ordinary Time starts with Pentecost and ends with Reign of Christ Sunday (The Sunday before Advent).

52. Ideas for Observing the Christian Calendar

When we choose to observe the Christian calendar, our life is immersed in light, life, and love. Our focus and our devotion are shifted from the world, from ourselves, toward Jesus. Our stories begin to conform to His Story, our lives to His Life. We live a Christ-centered rhythm.

On the following pages is a list of possible options for celebrating the days and seasons of the Christian calendar. If you choose to celebrate the calendar one time or several, make each year meaningful by selecting options that speak to your soul. Directions and/or explanations can be found for many of these ideas by searching the internet.

The Cycle of Light
(Celebrating the Incarnation—God with Us)

Advent: The season of thoughtful reflection and repentance.

1. First Sunday of Advent—Wait (Four Sundays before Christmas Day)
   - Make or purchase an Advent wreath.
   - Light the first candle of the advent wreath on this evening (purple—repentance).
   - Say a short prayer when lighting the candle.
   - Read and meditate on Psalm 130:5–6 (NASB)

     I wait for the LORD, *my soul does wait,*
     And in His word do I hope.
     My soul waits *for the* LORD
     More than the watchmen for the morning;
     Indeed, more than the watchmen for the morning.

   - Follow a schedule of daily Advent readings.
   - Incorporate a purchased or handmade Advent calendar into your celebration.
   - For younger children, use the Countdown to Jesus' Birthday Advent Calendar.
   - Make an Advent paper chain.
   - Participate in an Advent service project individually, as a family, or with friends.
   - Decide on the recipient of a family gift. Provide "shepherd's pouches" for each family member so each can "save" money to be given toward the gift.

2. **Second Sunday of Advent**—Prepare
   - Light an additional candle on this evening (purple—repentance).
   - Read and meditate this week on Luke 1:76–79 (NASB)

     "And you, child, will be called the prophet of the Most High;
     For you will go on BEFORE THE LORD TO PREPARE HIS WAYS;
     To give to His people the knowledge of salvation
     By the forgiveness of their sins,
     Because of the tender mercy of our God,
     With which the Sunrise from on high will visit us,
     TO SHINE UPON THOSE WHO SIT IN DARKNESS AND THE SHADOW OF DEATH, To guide our feet into the way of peace."

3. **Third Sunday of Advent**—Rejoice
   - Light an additional candle on the Advent wreath (pink—joy).
   - Read and mediate on Luke 1:46–49 (NASB)

     And Mary said:
     "My soul exalts the Lord,
     And my spirit has rejoiced in God my Savior.
     "For He has had regard for the humble state of His bondslave;
     For behold, from this time on all generations will count me blessed.
     For the Mighty One has done great things for me;
     And Holy is His name."

   - Send an annual Christmas letter (a way of reflecting on the past year). Joyfully notice the ways God has been present and faithful in your life and the way you have been able to be part of God's work in your corner of the world.

4. **Fourth Sunday of Advent**—Love
   - Light an additional candle on the Advent wreath (purple).
   - Read and meditate on John 3:16 (NASB).

     For God so loved the world, that He gave His only begotten Son, that whoever believes in Him shall not perish, but have eternal life.

5. December 24—Christmas Eve
    - Light the Christ candle in the center of the Advent wreath (white).
    - Hold a special family worship time. If your family has chosen to purchase a family "gift for Jesus," place the shepherd's pouches beside the manger of a special nativity scene. (Choose another time if all your family is not able to be together now.)
    - Hold a birthday celebration for Jesus on Christmas Eve or Christmas Day.

Christmas: The Season of Celebration and Wonder.

6. December 25—Christmas Day (The Twelve Days of Christmas Begin)
    - Light the white Christ candle in the center of your Advent wreath to mark the coming of the Light. Continue to light it each evening during Christmas.
    - Purchase twelve ornaments, one for each day of Christmas. Each ornament could represent a name of Jesus and have a Scripture passage that corresponds to it. Every evening during Christmas, choose an ornament, hang it on the Advent wreath or your tree and read the Scripture.
    - Invite someone who is alone or far from home to Christmas Dinner. Consider also possibly inviting someone to dinner on one of the twelve days of Christmas.
    - Keep your tree and decorations up until the end of the season on January 6th.
    - Send Christmas cards during the twelve days of Christmas.
    - Celebrate with twelve days of Christmas gift giving—provide toys, school supplies, or personal care products for disadvantaged children.
    - Volunteer at a soup kitchen.
    - Surprise your mail carrier, elderly neighbor, and others with inexpensive yet meaningful gifts.

7. December 26—Boxing Day (In honor of Stephen—Acts 6-8)
    - Volunteer at a soup kitchen, food bank, or homeless shelter.

8. January 1—New Year's Day (coincides with the Feast of the Holy Name)
    - Sometime during the day meditate on His name, sing praises to His name, speak it or reflect upon it.

9. January 5—Eve of Epiphany
    - Host a Twelfth Night party.

Epiphany: A celebration of the coming of God the Son for the whole earth.

10. **January 6**—Epiphany Begins
    - Consider: How do I want to be a witness of the Light of the World during this season? How will the Light spread?
    - Leave the porch light on or use electric candles in the windows as a concrete reminder.
    - Take down your Christmas tree and decorations, providing an intentional ending to the Christmas season.
    - Host a house blessing. Mark the lintel of the most used door in your home "20 C+M+B +__ (fill in the last two digits of the current calendar year)" in chalk. (These letters abbreviate the Latin phrase *Christus mansionem benedicat*, "May Christ bless the house.")
    - Invite a few people to study about Jesus with you through a four- to six-week informal, investigative Bible study.
    - Read an entire Gospel one or more times from start to finish, absorbing the full narrative sweep of Christ's remarkable life.
    - Read a book to sharpen your thinking about sharing your faith.
    - Gather a few friends and serve together in a volunteer opportunity.
    - Choose friends, coworkers, family members to pray for during Epiphany.
    - If someone appears open, invite her for coffee and some conversation about spiritual matters.
    - Give a friend a thoughtful book on the Christian faith.
    - Traditionally, Epiphany ends on the Sunday prior to Ash Wednesday.

The Cycle of Life

(Contemplating Salvation—God for Us)

Lent: A season of darkness; humbled in the turning. A time to prepare.

11. Ash Wednesday

- Fast—create space in your life for your relationship with God.
- Prayerful reading and study of Scripture.
    - Read the Crucifixion account in each Gospel.
    - Read the same Crucifixion account in multiple versions of the Bible.
- Choose a thoughtful book to read during the season of Lent. Below are some suggestions:
    - *The Incomparable Christ*, J. Oswald Sanders
    - *Jesus, Keep Me Near the Cross*, Nancy Guthrie
    - *The View from Mount Calvary: 24 Portraits of the Cross throughout Scripture*, John Phillips
    - *The Pleasures of God*, John Piper
    - *The Man Born to be King*, Dorothy L. Sayers
    - *Walk with Jesus*, Charles Swindoll
- For younger children, use *Lenten Lights* by Noel Piper for Lenten devotions.
- Repent—create space in your life to hear the voice of God speaking to your heart.
- Practice charity. With money saved by fasting from something of choice, provide for a charitable organization, a person, or family in need.
- Refrain from having flowers in your home during the season of Lent.
- Lenten Cross—contains seven purple candles, one for each of the Sundays of Lent and one for Maundy Thursday. Extinguish one candle each week, entering ever more deeply into the darkness that will culminate in Christ's death. Light all candles each evening of the first week or one day that week. Extinguish one candle each week of Lent. The last candle should be extinguished on Maundy Thursday (usually the center one).

- Incorporate a visual or tangible symbol into your observance.
    › Carry a two-inch nail in your pocket during Lent.
    › Wear a cross around your neck, perhaps hidden beneath your clothing.
    › Place a cross in a noticeable spot within your home.
    › Fill your home with reproductions of art on the subject.
    › Place a palm branch through your door knocker or somewhere else in your home on Palm Sunday.

The Paschal Triduum: Make provision for spiritual engagement with God.

- Consider a no-fire fast during the triduum (a reminder that the Light has gone out of the world).

12. Maundy Thursday
- Spend time alone each day reading, meditating, and praying.
- Engage in a Journey to the Cross or Way of the Cross, a series of stations representing particular moments in the Passion of Christ.

13. Good Friday
- If possible, take the day off work.
- Meditate on the Seven Last Words of Christ or choose just one to meditate on throughout the day.

14. Holy Saturday (also called Silent Saturday, representing the silence of the tomb)
- Keep it a quiet day.
- Read/explore the Apostle's Creed.
- Bake Easter Cookies.

Easter: A season of joy. The celebration of Christ's resurrection.

15. Easter Sunday
- Make it festive.
- Take a predawn walk. Watch the sun rise. Contemplate the amazing reality of resurrection and feel the incredible joy and wonder of Easter.
- Greet family, friends, and people at church with, "Christ is risen!" ("He is risen indeed!")
- On Easter Day and through the Easter season, go crazy with flowers in your home.

- Light a white candle during your Easter meal.
- Before church on Easter morning, read one of the Gospel accounts of the resurrection and maybe 1 Corinthians 15 or Romans 8.
- Play joyous music in your home on Easter morning.

16. Easter Season
- Host a different group of friends for dinner each week during the season.
- Go to lunch with a group of fellow worshipers after church each Sunday of Easter.
- Possibly allow yourself some culinary treats that you normally limit in your diet.
- Ask Jesus to renew one part of your "self" over the weeks of Easter:
    › less doubt and more faith
    › less procrastination and more discipline
    › less irritability and more patience
    › less lying and more honesty
    › less indulgence and more generosity. Our hearts are transformed over time. God causes the growth (John 15:5).
- Consider incorporating visual or tangible symbols into your observance:
    › Place a simple, painted wooden egg or other symbol in a place you will see each morning while dressing.
    › Designate a spot in your home for displaying small prints or photographs that represent the current season.
    › Place fresh flowers on a table through the season of new life.
    › Get outdoors into the resurgence of the spring landscape.

17. The Feast of the Ascension of Our Lord—Forty days after Easter, always celebrated on a Thursday

- Take some time in retreat.
- Invite a small group of friends for dinner to celebrate the completion of Christ's work on our behalf.
- Meditate on the exaltation of Christ to glory.

The Cycle of Love

(Concentrating on the outworking love of redemption—God through us)

Ordinary Time: A six month long season beginning with Pentecost (50th and final day of Easter) and ending with Reign of Christ Sunday (the Sunday before Advent).

18. Pentecost—The culmination of the Easter season and a time to celebrate the outpouring and indwelling of the third Person of the Trinity. Pentecost is generally celebrated for eight days, from Sunday to Sunday.

   - Wear red to church on Pentecost.
   - Through the eight days of Pentecost, light a red candle at your household meal each day.
   - Locate a dove and set it out during the Octave of Pentecost.

19. Ordinary Time—Christ works in us and through us by His Spirit (Luke 24 and Acts 1).

   - Light a green candle during mealtime.
   - Study the Holy Spirit.
   - Study the Trinity.
   - Proclaim the Good News.
   - Breathe a breath prayer. Pay attention to where God might be present in that moment and be mindful of your desire to keep your eyes and heart turned toward Christ.
   - Breathe a simple breath prayer each time you perform some routine activity such as washing your hands or getting in your car.

53. Christian Calendar Planning Form

Use this form in conjunction with "Ideas for Observing the Christian Calendar" to plan your family's observance of the Christian year.

The Cycle of Light

(Celebrating the Incarnation—God with Us)

If you or your family choose to "give a gift to Jesus" as part of your Christmas celebration, be sure to do the following prior to Christmas.

November or Early December

- Choose the recipient of the Jesus gift from your family. _____
- Decide on the amount to be spent (percentage of gift expenditures, coffee money, etc.). _____
- Be sure everyone has a shepherd's pouch or other container for collecting money.

Advent: The season of thoughtful reflection and repentance.

1. First Sunday of Advent—Wait (purple)

   _____
   _____
   _____

2. Second Sunday of Advent—Prepare (purple)

   _____
   _____
   _____

3. Third Sunday of Advent—Rejoice (pink)

_____
_____
_____

4. Fourth Sunday of Advent—Love (purple)

_____
_____
_____

5. December 24—Christmas Eve (white)

_____
_____
_____

Christmas: The Season of Celebration and Wonder.

6. December 25—Christmas Day (The Twelve Days of Christmas Begin)

_____
_____
_____

7. December 26—Boxing Day (in honor of Stephen—Acts 6—8)

_____
_____
_____

8. January 1—New Year's Day (coincides with the Feast of the Holy Name)

_____

_____

_____

9. January 5—Eve of Epiphany

_____

_____

_____

Epiphany: A time to both inhabit the Story and tell the Story.

10. January 6—Epiphany Begins

_____

_____

_____

Final Sunday of Epiphany (the Sunday prior to Ash Wednesday)

_____

_____

_____

The Cycle of Life

(Contemplating Salvation—God for Us)

Lent: A season of darkness; humbled in the turning. A time to prepare.

11. Ash Wednesday

_____

_____

_____

The Paschal Triduum: A time for spiritual engagement with God.

12. Maundy Thursday

_____

_____

_____

13. Good Friday

_____

_____

_____

14. Holy Saturday

_____

_____

_____

Easter: A season of joy. The celebration of Christ's resurrection.

15. Easter Sunday

_____
_____
_____

16. Easter Season (50 days)

_____
_____
_____

17. The Feast of the Ascension of Our Lord (fortieth day after Easter/Thursday)

_____
_____
_____

The Cycle of Love
(Concentrating on the outworking love of redemption—God through us)

Ordinary Time: A time for focusing on all aspects of the ministry and mission of Jesus Christ who is Himself working in us and through us.

Pentecost: A time to celebrate the outpouring and indwelling of the third Person of the Trinity.

18. Pentecost (fiftieth day after Easter)

_____

_____

_____

19. Ordinary Time—Christ works in us and through us by his Spirit.

_____

_____

_____

54. Fasting

Christian fasting is the voluntary denial of food (or some other regularly enjoyed pleasure) for a specific period of time. Additionally, a Christian fast is always entered into for spiritual purposes. Much like the practice of observing the Sabbath, observing a fast creates space for God.

"And when you fast, do not look gloomy like the hypocrites, for they disfigure their faces that their fasting may be seen by others. Truly, I say to you, they have received their reward. But when you fast, anoint your head and wash your face, that your fasting may not be seen by others but by your Father who is in secret. And your Father who sees in secret will reward you."

(Matthew 6:16-18)

Unlike other types of fasting (medical, dieting, etc.), Biblical fasting is not for the benefit of your physical health. It is done for the purpose of seeking to know God more intimately. Fasting can be a time of drawing nearer to God through prayer and/or confession.

There are several biblical examples of fasting, including:

- Daniel (Daniel 1:8–16; 10:2–3)
- Jesus (Luke 4:2)
- Saul (Acts 9:9)
- The early church (Acts 13:2)

We can read about fasting, but the only way to truly understand the value of fasting is to practice it. As you gain experience with fasting you will discover how dramatically it helps turn your focus toward God, deepen your relationship with Him, and nourish your soul.

3 Types of Fasts

1. A partial fast—restricting the diet by either cutting out certain foods or cutting out certain meals (Daniel 10:3).

2. A normal fast—eating no food but drinking liquids, either water or juice. After two to three days of normal fasting, a person enters a physiological state called ketosis, which often coincides with heightened spiritual awareness (Luke 4:2).

3. An absolute fast—consuming nothing at all. This type of fast would, of course, be limited to no more than a day or two (Ezra 10:6; Esther 4:16; Acts 9:9).

Strictly speaking, fasting in the Bible means to go without eating or drinking. We can, however, appropriately extend the concept to other activities and substances, especially if there are medical reasons that we should not engage in a fast from food. In our culture of consumerism, the practice of abstaining from certain things for specified periods can help us loosen our hold and turn our focus from what we see with our physical eyes to our Lord and Savior and what truly matters.

> In a more tangible, visceral way than any other spiritual discipline, fasting reveals our excessive attachments and the assumptions that lie behind them.... Fasting brings us face to face with how we put the material world ahead of its spiritual Source.[48]
>
> Marjorie J. Thompson

The Benefits of Prayer and Fasting

When God calls us to prayer and fasting, He always does so for our benefit. The Scriptures point out at least seven benefits to prayer and fasting.

1. *Our attitudes, feelings, and thoughts get sifted, pruned and purified so that God might entrust us with a greater ministry.* By fasting and praying, we become more disciplined toward the things of the Father. We give Him opportunity to cut away from us those things that will slow us down, do us in, or keep us from His plans and purposes.

2. *We are able to discern more clearly the will of God for our lives.* Fasting clears our spiritual eyes and ears so we can accurately discern what God desires to reveal to us.

3. *We are confronted with our sins and shortcomings so we might confess them to God, receive forgiveness for them, and walk in greater righteousness.* Many times we break stubborn, sinful habits when we fast and pray. Fasting and prayer cleanse us and purify us from the errors that have kept us entangled in sin and folly.

4. *We experience a release of supernatural power.* Genuine fasting and prayer result in spiritual growth, including a renewed outpouring of supernatural power. Certain problems and situations cannot be resolved apart from fasting and prayer.

5. *We can influence national issues and concerns through our prayers.* As we fast and pray for our nation, God will move. He will pour out His Spirit, in His ways and in His timing. We can count on it.

6. *We can help build up God's people.* Prayer is the generator of the church. It gives power to its ministers. It propels outreach to the lost. It creates a climate in which evangelistic efforts succeed.

7. *Our minds are sharpened.* When we fast and pray, we begin to understand the Scriptures as never before. We become sensitive to God's timing and direction, with an increased awareness and ability to discern. We become keenly aware of what God desires to do and accomplish not only in our lives, but also in the lives of those around us.[49]

55. Fasting for Beginners

"Fasting is voluntarily going without food—or any other regularly enjoyed, good gift from God—for the sake of some spiritual purpose. It is markedly counter-cultural in our consumerist society, like abstaining from sex until marriage."[50]

David Mathis

How to Start Fasting

1. Start small.
If fasting has not been part of your life experience, don't jump right in to a weeklong fast. Begin with a one meal fast. Try one meal a week for several weeks. After that you might try two meals a week. Eventually, you may decide to work your way up to a daylong fast or a two-day juice fast.

When observing a juice fast, one abstains from all food and beverage, except for juice and water. Juice provides nutrients and sugar that help the body keep operating. During a juice fast the effects of going without solid food are still felt.

It is not recommended that you abstain from water during a fast of any length.

2. Plan.
Fasting is a spiritual discipline for simplicity; total surrender to God, a singularity of heart. It is not merely an act of self-denial. As such, we should have a plan for what we will do during our normal meal time. Fasting creates space for prayer, meditation, self-reflection, or some other act of love and devotion.

Before plunging haphazardly into your first fast, develop a plan. Each fast you undertake should have a specific spiritual purpose. Connect your plan to your purpose. Based on your purpose, design a focus for the time you would have spent eating. Remember: spiritual fasting requires a purpose and plan. Otherwise, it's just a missed meal.

3. Consider others.
Think about how your fast will affect others. Don't use it as an excuse to be unloving to others. Proper fasting exhibits love both vertically and horizontally.

If you have regular meal times with others, evaluate how your abstaining from the meal will affect them. Let them know ahead of time that you will not be eating. Avoid springing it on them at the last minute or being a no-show.

4. Mix it up.
A variety of forms of fasting are found in the Bible. The most common type is private and partial fasting. Personal and communal, private and public, congregational and national, regular and occasional, absolute and partial fasting are also mentioned.

Consider fasting with others such as your family, small group, or church. Fast together for some shared need requiring God's wisdom and guidance. Seek His intervention together during times of great difficulty. In addition to your private fasting, it is important to fast publically with other believers.

5. Think outside the meal.
When we hear the term "fasting," we tend to think of food, but fasting from food is not necessarily for everyone. Health conditions must be considered. Not everyone is physically able to abstain from food.

Martyn Lloyd-Jones says, "Fasting should really be made to include abstinence from anything which is legitimate in and of itself for the sake of some special spiritual purpose."

If health concerns prohibit a food fast, consider fasting from some regular form of enjoyment in order to spend time focused on enjoying God. Other fasts might include smart phones, social media, computers, television, binge watching, movie theaters, shopping, or coffee shops. In 1 Corinthians 7:5, Paul even talks about married couples fasting from sex "for a limited time" in order to devote themselves more fully to God.

6. Turn your attention to Jesus.
When those stomach growls come, don't dwell on them. Go to your plan and turn your attention to Jesus. Be filled with Him.

56. Tips for Engaging in the Spiritual Practice of Fasting

Consider fasting from:

- Desserts and sweets
- Processed foods
- Chocolate
- Expensive cups of coffee
- Buying books
- Reading books and magazines
- Watching television
- Listening to music
- Going to the theater or viewing movies
- Shopping
- Wearing colorful jewelry
- Applying make-up
- Social media

A few ways to focus your prayers during a fast:

- Meditate on a verse or passage of Scripture. Cultivate your hunger for God as you continually turn your thoughts from physical hunger to your deeper hunger for God and His Word.
- Watch and pray. Use your experience to rely on Jesus as your Source rather than relying on overeating, overworking, overspending, judging others, etc.
- Intercede. Engage in concentrated prayer for someone in need.
- Seek. Have a decision to make? Go to God for discernment.
- Practice:
    - Relying on the Holy Spirit rather than yourself and your own abilities.
    - Serving those who are spiritually and/or physically hungry.
    - Doing all for the glory of God.

57. Scriptures for Fasting

A Selection of Scripture for Meditation

Psalm 27:4, 8
One thing have I asked of the Lord, that will I seek after: that I may dwell in the house of the Lord all the days of my life, to gaze upon the beauty of the Lord and to inquire in his temple.... You have said, "Seek my face." My heart says to you, "Your face, Lord, do I seek."

Psalm 42:1–2
As a deer pants for flowing streams, so pants my soul for you, O God. My soul thirsts for God, for the living God. When shall I come and appear before God?

Psalm 57:8–10
Awake, my glory! Awake, O harp and lyre! I will awake the dawn! I will give thanks to you, O Lord, among the peoples; I will sing praises to you among the nations. For your steadfast love is great to the heavens, your faithfulness to the clouds.

Psalm 62:5–8
For God alone, O my soul, wait in silence, for my hope is from him. He only is my rock and my salvation, my fortress; I shall not be shaken. On God rests my salvation and my glory; my mighty rock, my refuge is God. Trust in him at all times, O people; pour out your heart before him; God is a refuge for us. Selah

Psalm 63:1–8
O God, you are my God; earnestly I seek you; my soul thirsts for you; my flesh faints for you, as in a dry and weary land where there is no water. So I have looked upon you in the sanctuary, beholding your power and glory. Because your steadfast love is better than life, my lips will praise you. So I will bless you as long as I live; in your name I will lift up my hands. My soul will be satisfied as with fat and rich food, and my mouth will praise you with joyful lips, when I remember you upon my bed, and meditate on you in the watches of the night; for you have been my help, and in the shadow of your wings I will sing for joy. My soul clings to you; your right hand upholds me.

Psalm 73:26–28
My flesh and my heart may fail, but God is the strength of my heart and my portion forever. For behold, those who are far from you shall perish; you put an end to everyone who is unfaithful to you. But for me it is good to be near God; I have made the Lord God my refuge, that I may tell of all your works.

Psalm 84:1–4, 10
How lovely is your dwelling place, O Lord of hosts! My soul longs, yes, faints for the courts of the Lord; my heart and flesh sing for joy to the living God. Even the sparrow finds a home, and the swallow a nest for herself, where she may lay her young, at your altars, O Lord of hosts, my King and my God. Blessed are those who dwell in your house, ever singing your praise! Selah.... For a day in your courts is better than a thousand elsewhere. I would rather be a doorkeeper in the house of my God than dwell in the tents of wickedness.

Psalm 108:1
My heart is steadfast, O God! I will sing and make melody with all my being!

Psalm 119:20, 81
My soul is consumed with longing for your rules at all times.... My soul longs for your salvation; I hope in your word.

Psalm 143:6
I stretch out my hands to you; my soul thirsts for you like a parched land. Selah

Matthew 4:4
But he answered, "It is written, 'Man shall not live by bread alone, but by every word that comes from the mouth of God.'"

Matthew 11:25–30
At that time Jesus declared, "I thank you, Father, Lord of heaven and earth, that you have hidden these things from the wise and understanding and revealed them to little children; yes, Father, for such was your gracious will. All things have been handed over to me by my Father, and no one knows the Son except the Father, and no one knows the Father except the Son and anyone to whom the Son chooses to reveal him. Come to me, all who labor and are heavy laden, and I will give you rest. Take my yoke upon you, and learn from me, for I am gentle and lowly in heart, and you will find rest for your souls. For my yoke is easy, and my burden is light."

John 1:1–8
In the beginning was the Word, and the Word was with God, and the Word was God. He was in the beginning with God. All things were made through him, and without him was not any thing made that was made. In him was life, and the life was the light of men. The light shines in the darkness, and the darkness has not overcome it. There was a man sent from God, whose name was John. He came as a witness, to bear witness about the light, that all might believe through him. He was not the light, but came to bear witness about the light.

John 6:33, 35
"For the bread of God is he who comes down from heaven and gives life to the world."… Jesus said to them, "I am the bread of life; whoever comes to me shall not hunger, and whoever believes in me shall never thirst."

John 8:32
"You will know the truth, and the truth will set you free."

Galatians 4:6
And because you are sons, God has sent the Spirit of his Son into our hearts, crying, "Abba! Father!"

Philippians 2:1–11
So if there is any encouragement in Christ, any comfort from love, any participation in the Spirit, any affection and sympathy, complete my joy by being of the same mind, having the same love, being in full accord and of one mind. Do nothing from selfish ambition or conceit, but in humility count others more significant than yourselves. Let each of you look not only to his own interests, but also to the interests of others. Have this mind among yourselves, which is yours in Christ Jesus, who, though he was in the form of God, did not count equality with God a thing to be grasped, but emptied himself, by taking the form of a servant, being born in the likeness of men. And being found in human form, he humbled himself by becoming obedient to the point of death, even death on a cross. Therefore God has highly exalted him and bestowed on him the name that is above every name, so that at the name of Jesus every knee should bow, in heaven and on earth and under the earth, and every tongue confess that Jesus Christ is Lord, to the glory of God the Father.

Philippians 3:7–14
But whatever gain I had, I counted as loss for the sake of Christ. Indeed, I count everything as loss because of the surpassing worth of knowing Christ Jesus my Lord. For his sake I have suffered the loss of all things and count them as rubbish, in order that I may gain Christ and be found in him, not having a righteousness of my own that comes from the law, but that which comes through faith in Christ, the righteousness from God that depends on faith—that I may know him and the power of his resurrection, and may share his sufferings, becoming like him in his death, that by any means possible I may attain the resurrection from the dead. Not that I have already obtained this or am already perfect, but I press on to make it my own, because Christ Jesus has made me his own. Brothers, I do not consider that I have made it my own. But one thing I do: forgetting what lies behind and straining forward to what lies ahead, I press on toward the goal for the prize of the upward call of God in Christ Jesus.

Colossians 1:15–23

He is the image of the invisible God, the firstborn of all creation. For by him all things were created, in heaven and on earth, visible and invisible, whether thrones or dominions or rulers or authorities—all things were created through him and for him. And he is before all things, and in him all things hold together. And he is the head of the body, the church. He is the beginning, the firstborn from the dead, that in everything he might be preeminent. For in him all the fullness of God was pleased to dwell, and through him to reconcile to himself all things, whether on earth or in heaven, making peace by the blood of his cross. And you, who once were alienated and hostile in mind, doing evil deeds, he has now reconciled in his body of flesh by his death, in order to present you holy and blameless and above reproach before him, if indeed you continue in the faith, stable and steadfast, not shifting from the hope of the gospel that you heard, which has been proclaimed in all creation under heaven, and of which I, Paul, became a minister.

Hebrews 1:1–4

Long ago, at many times and in many ways, God spoke to our fathers by the prophets, but in these last days he has spoken to us by his Son, whom he appointed the heir of all things, through whom also he created the world. He is the radiance of the glory of God and the exact imprint of his nature, and he upholds the universe by the word of his power. After making purification for sins, he sat down at the right hand of the Majesty on high, having become as much superior to angels as the name he has inherited is more excellent than theirs.

1 Peter 2:4–10

As you come to him, a living stone rejected by men but in the sight of God chosen and precious, you yourselves like living stones are being built up as a spiritual house, to be a holy priesthood, to offer spiritual sacrifices acceptable to God through Jesus Christ. For it stands in Scripture: "Behold, I am laying in Zion a stone, a cornerstone chosen and precious, and whoever believes in him will not be put to shame." So the honor is for you who believe, but for those who do not believe, "The stone that the builders rejected has become the cornerstone," and "A stone of stumbling, and a rock of offense." They stumble because they disobey the word, as they were destined to do. But you are a chosen race, a royal priesthood, a holy nation, a people for his own possession, that you may proclaim the excellencies of him who called you out of darkness into his marvelous light. Once you were not a people, but now you are God's people; once you had not received mercy, but now you have received mercy.[51]

58. Gratitude Scripture Challenge

This Scripture Challenge is extremely versatile. Use the list of Scriptures in whatever way works best with your personal schedule and unique God-wiring. Read the Scriptures daily or write them out by hand. Meditate on them. Journal, Verse Map, or Pray them in Color. Choose one or more and memorize them.

DAY	SCRIPTURE
1	Colossians 3:17, Psalm 136:2–3, Psalm 136:26, Psalm 118:28
2	Psalm 95:2, Luke 17:16
3	Psalm 138:1, Psalm 9:1, Psalm 86:12
4	Isaiah 38:19, Psalm 145:10
5	Psalm 79:13
6	Psalm 108:3, Psalm 109:30, Psalm 111:1
7	Psalm 116:17
8	James 1:17
9	1 Chronicles 16:34, Psalm 107:1
10	Psalm 7:17
11	Psalm 106:1, Psalm 118:1, Psalm 118:29, Psalm 136:1
12	Revelation 11:17
13	Revelation 4:9
14	Psalm 30:4, Psalm 54:6, Psalm 92:1, Psalm 97:12, Psalm 75:1
15	2 Corinthians 9:15, John 4:10
16	Acts 2:38, Acts 10:45
17	Hebrews 4:12
18	Psalm 65:2
19	Ephesians 2:8–9, Ephesians 4:7, Romans 3:24
20	Romans 6:23
21	Colossians 1:14
22	Romans 5:15–17
23	Luke 22:19, 1 Corinthians 11:24
24	Romans 6:17
25	Psalm 28:7
26	1 Corinthians 15:57
27	Colossians 1:12
28	1 Timothy 2:1, 2 Thessalonians 1:3, Ephesians 1:15–16
29	1 Timothy 4:4, Ephesians 5:20
30	Philippians 4:6, 1 Thessalonians 5:18

59. Scripture Praise A–Z

Praise the Lord God for who He is…

A. **Almighty God.** *O Lord God of hosts, who is mighty as you are, O Lord, with your faithfulness all around you?* (Psalm 89:8).

B. **The Banner Who Leads in Triumphal Procession.** *But thanks be to God, who in Christ always leads us in triumphal procession, and through us spreads the fragrance of the knowledge of him everywhere* (2 Corinthians 2:14).

C. **Creator God.** *"You are the Lord, you alone. You have made heaven, the heaven of heavens, with all their host, the earth and all that is on it, the seas and all that is in them; and you preserve all of them; and the host of heaven worships you"* (Nehemiah 9:6).

D. **Deliverer.** *But I am poor and needy; hasten to me, O God! You are my help and my deliverer; O Lord, do not delay!* (Psalm 70:5).

E. **Everlasting Father.** *For to us a child is born, to us a son is given; and the government shall be upon his shoulder, and his name shall be called Wonderful Counselor, Mighty God, Everlasting Father, Prince of Peace* (Isaiah 9:6).

F. **Faithful.** *The steadfast love of the Lord never ceases; his mercies never come to an end; they are new every morning; great is your faithfulness* (Lamentations 3:22–23).

G. **Good.** *You are good and do good; teach me your statutes* (Psalm 119:68).

H. **The Holy God.** *And the four living creatures, each of them with six wings, are full of eyes all around and within, and day and night they never cease to say, "Holy, holy, holy, is the Lord God Almighty, who was and is and is to come!"* (Revelation 4:8).

I. **Immeasurable.** *Oh, the depth of the riches and wisdom and knowledge of God! How unsearchable are his judgments and how inscrutable his ways!* (Romans 11:33).

J. **Justifier of the One Who Has Faith.** *It was to show his righteousness at the present time, so that he might be just and the justifier of the one who has faith in Jesus* (Romans 3:26).

K. **King of Kings and Lord of Lords.** *…[H]e who is the blessed and only Sovereign, the King of kings and Lord of lords* (1 Timothy 6:15).

L. **Love.** *So we have come to know and to believe the love that God has for us. God is love, and whoever abides in love abides in God, and God abides in him* (1 John 4:16).

M. **Full of Mercy.** *Nevertheless, in your great mercies you did not make an end of them or forsake them, for you are a gracious and merciful God* (Nehemiah 9:31).

N. **Near.** *The LORD is near to all who call on him, to all who call on him in truth* (Psalm 145:18).

O. **The One Who Gave His Only Son.** *For God so loved the world, that he gave his only Son, that whoever believes in him should not perish but have eternal life* (John 3:16).

P. **Provider of All Things.** *And God is able to make all grace abound to you, so that having all sufficiency in all things at all times, you may abound in every good work* (2 Corinthians 9:8).

Q. **In the Quiet.** *And after the earthquake a fire, but the LORD was not in the fire. And after the fire the sound of a low whisper* (1 Kings 19:12).

R. **My Refuge.** *He only is my rock and my salvation, my fortress; I shall not be shaken. On God rests my salvation and my glory; my mighty rock, my refuge is God* (Psalm 62:6–7).

S. **Our Savior.** *To the only God, our Savior, through Jesus Christ our Lord, be glory, majesty, dominion, and authority, before all time and now and forever. Amen* (Jude 25).

T. **Transcendent.** *The LORD is high above all nations, and his glory above the heavens!* (Psalm 113:4).

U. **Unbound by Place or Time.** *Where shall I go from your Spirit? Or where shall I flee from your presence? If I ascend to heaven, you are there! If I make my bed in Sheol, you are there! If I take the wings of the morning and dwell in the uttermost parts of the sea, even there your hand shall lead me, and your right hand shall hold me. If I say, "Surely the darkness shall cover me, and the light about me be night," even the darkness is not dark to you; the night is bright as the day, for darkness is as light with you* (Psalm 139:7-12).

V. **The Victorious One.** *When the perishable puts on the imperishable, and the mortal puts on immortality, then shall come to pass the saying that is written: "Death is swallowed up in victory. O death, where is your victory? O death, where is your sting?" The sting of death is sin, and the power of sin is the law. But thanks be to God, who gives us the victory through our Lord Jesus Christ* (1 Corinthians 15:54–57).

W. **Worthy of our Worship.** "Worthy are you, our Lord and God, to receive glory and honor and power, for you created all things, and by your will they existed and were created" (Revelation 4:11).

X. **EXtravagant.** *In him we have redemption through his blood, the forgiveness of our trespasses, according to the riches of his grace, which he lavished upon us, in all wisdom and insight making known to us the mystery of his will, according to his purpose, which he set forth in Christ as a plan for the fullness of time, to unite all things in him, things in heaven and things on earth* (Ephesians 1:7-10).

Y. **The Deepest Yearning of My Soul.** *My soul longs, yes, faints for the courts of the Lord; my heart and flesh sing for joy to the living God* (Psalm 84:2).

Z. **Zealous.** *The Lord goes out like a mighty man, like a man of war he stirs up his zeal; he cries out, he shouts aloud, he shows himself mighty against his foes* (Isaiah 42:13).

60. Seventeen Attributes of God

1. **Love** – God has made me His child (1 John 3:1).

2. **Eternality** – God never runs out of resources (Psalm 90:2).

3. **Presence** – God is always with me (Hebrews 13:5).

4. **Immutability** – God never changes His action towards me (James 1:17).

5. **Self-Sufficiency** – God is not dependent on others for my life (Exodus 3:14).

6. **Wisdom** – God gives me wisdom to live successfully (1 Corinthians 1:20–26).

7. **Omnipotence** – God is strong enough to care for me (Jeremiah 32:17).

8. **Patience** – God waits for me to change to be like Him (2 Peter 3:9).

9. **Truth** – God has absolute standards for me (Numbers 23:19).

10. **Grace** – God is compassionate towards me (Ephesians 2:4).

11. **Faithfulness** – God can be trusted to provide for me (2 Timothy 2:13).

12. **Jealousy** – God is "fanatical" in His protection of me (Exodus 34:14).

13. **Righteousness** – God will do what is right concerning me (Romans 2:6).

14. **Holiness** – God provides guidelines for pure living (Leviticus 19, Isaiah 6:3).

15. **Goodness** – God generously gives to me (Psalm 86:5).

16. **Sovereignty** – God graciously directs every event of life (Ephesians 1:11).

17. **Omniscience** – God knows all I need to live successfully (Psalm 139:1).[52]

61. My Father...

- **Loves me** – John 3:16
- **Cares for me** – Matthew 6:26
- **Forgives me** – Psalm 103:12
- **Is compassionate** – Psalm 103:4–5
- **Is giving** – Romans 8:32
- **Is understanding** – Psalm 139:1–2
- **Is accepting** – Psalm 139:1–6
- **Satisfies** – Psalm 107:9
- **Persistently pursues me** – Luke 19:10
- **Is reason** – Isaiah 1:18
- **Pardons** – Psalm 103:3
- **Heals** – Isaiah 53:5
- **Redeems** – Job 19:25
- **Is loving-kindness** – Psalm 86:15
- **Renews** – Isaiah 40:31
- **Is righteous** – Jeremiah 9:23–24
- **Is gracious** – Ephesians 1:7–8
- **Is sovereign** – Psalm 103:19[53]

62. God's Words of Love

Deuteronomy 7:9
Know therefore that the Lord your God is God, the faithful God who keeps covenant and steadfast love with those who love him and keep his commandments, to a thousand generations.

Psalm 16:11
You make known to me the path of life; in your presence there is fullness of joy; at your right hand are pleasures forevermore.

Psalm 36:5
Your steadfast love, O Lord, extends to the heavens, your faithfulness to the clouds.

Psalm 63:3
Because your steadfast love is better than life, my lips will praise you.

Psalm 66:16–20
Come and hear, all you who fear God, and I will tell what he has done for my soul. I cried to him with my mouth, and high praise was on my tongue. If I had cherished iniquity in my heart, the Lord would not have listened. But truly God has listened; he has attended to the voice of my prayer. Blessed be God, because he has not rejected my prayer or removed his steadfast love from me!

Psalm 73:24–26
You guide me with your counsel, and afterward you will receive me to glory. Whom have I in heaven but you? And there is nothing on earth that I desire besides you. My flesh and my heart may fail, but God is the strength of my heart and my portion forever.

Psalm 86:15
But you, O Lord, are a God merciful and gracious, slow to anger and abounding in steadfast love and faithfulness.

Psalm 89:1–2
I will sing of the steadfast love of the Lord, forever; with my mouth I will make known your faithfulness to all generations. For I said, "Steadfast love will be built up forever; in the heavens you will establish your faithfulness."

Psalm 94:17–19

If the LORD had not been my help, my soul would soon have lived in the land of silence. When I thought, "My foot slips," your steadfast love, O LORD, held me up. When the cares of my heart are many, your consolations cheer my soul.

Psalm 107:8–9

Let them thank the LORD for his steadfast love, for his wondrous works to the children of man! For he satisfies the longing soul, and the hungry soul he fills with good things.

Psalm 136:26

Give thanks to the God of heaven, for his steadfast love endures forever.

Psalm 143:8

Let me hear in the morning of your steadfast love, for in you I trust. Make me know the way I should go, for to you I lift up my soul.

Song of Solomon 2:10, 14

My beloved speaks and says to me: "Arise, my love, my beautiful one, and come away…. O my dove, in the clefts of the rock, in the crannies of the cliff, let me see your face, let me hear your voice, for your voice is sweet, and your face is lovely."

Isaiah 54:10

"For the mountains may depart and the hills be removed, but my steadfast love shall not depart from you, and my covenant of peace shall not be removed," says the LORD, who has compassion on you.

Jeremiah 29:11–13

For I know the plans I have for you, declares the LORD, plans for welfare and not for evil, to give you a future and a hope. Then you will call upon me and come and pray to me, and I will hear you. You will seek me and find me, when you seek me with all your heart.

Lamentations 3:21–26

But this I call to mind, and therefore I have hope: The steadfast love of the LORD never ceases; his mercies never come to an end; they are new every morning; great is your faithfulness. "The LORD is my portion," says my soul, "therefore I will hope in him." The LORD is good to those who wait for him, to the soul who seeks him. It is good that one should wait quietly for the salvation of the LORD.

Zephaniah 3:17
The Lord your God is in your midst, a mighty one who will save; he will rejoice over you with gladness; he will quiet you by his love; he will exult over you with loud singing.

Mark 12:28–31
And one of the scribes came up and heard them disputing with one another, and seeing that he answered them well, asked him, "Which commandment is the most important of all?" Jesus answered, "The most important is, 'Hear, O Israel: The Lord our God, the Lord is one. And you shall love the Lord your God with all your heart and with all your soul and with all your mind and with all your strength.' The second is this: 'You shall love your neighbor as yourself.' There is no other commandment greater than these."

John 3:16
"For God so loved the world, that he gave his only Son, that whoever believes in him should not perish but have eternal life."

John 15:9–11
"As the Father has loved me, so have I loved you. Abide in my love. If you keep my commandments, you will abide in my love, just as I have kept my Father's commandments and abide in his love. These things I have spoken to you, that my joy may be in you, and that your joy may be full."

Romans 5:2–5
Through him we have also obtained access by faith into this grace in which we stand, and we rejoice in hope of the glory of God. Not only that, but we rejoice in our sufferings, knowing that suffering produces endurance, and endurance produces character, and character produces hope, and hope does not put us to shame, because God's love has been poured into our hearts through the Holy Spirit who has been given to us.

Romans 5:8
But God shows his love for us in that while we were still sinners, Christ died for us.

Romans 8:35–39
Who shall separate us from the love of Christ? Shall tribulation, or distress, or persecution, or famine, or nakedness, or danger, or sword? As it is written, "For your sake we are being killed all the day long; we are regarded as sheep to be slaughtered." No, in all these things we are more than conquerors through him who loved us. For I am sure that neither death nor life, nor angels nor rulers, nor things present nor things to come, nor powers, nor height nor depth, nor anything else in all creation, will be able to separate us from the love of God in Christ Jesus our Lord.

Galatians 2:20

I have been crucified with Christ. It is no longer I who live, but Christ who lives in me. And the life I now live in the flesh I live by faith in the Son of God, who loved me and gave himself for me.

Ephesians 2:4–7

But God, being rich in mercy, because of the great love with which he loved us, even when we were dead in our trespasses, made us alive together with Christ—by grace you have been saved—and raised us up with him and seated us with him in the heavenly places in Christ Jesus, so that in the coming ages he might show the immeasurable riches of his grace in kindness toward us in Christ Jesus.

Ephesians 3:16–21

[T]hat according to the riches of his glory he may grant you to be strengthened with power through his Spirit in your inner being, so that Christ may dwell in your hearts through faith—that you, being rooted and grounded in love, may have strength to comprehend with all the saints what is the breadth and length and height and depth, and to know the love of Christ that surpasses knowledge, that you may be filled with all the fullness of God. Now to him who is able to do far more abundantly than all that we ask or think, according to the power at work within us, to him be glory in the church and in Christ Jesus throughout all generations, forever and ever. Amen.

1 Peter 1:3–9

Blessed be the God and Father of our Lord Jesus Christ! According to his great mercy, he has caused us to be born again to a living hope through the resurrection of Jesus Christ from the dead, to an inheritance that is imperishable, undefiled, and unfading, kept in heaven for you, who by God's power are being guarded through faith for a salvation ready to be revealed in the last time. In this you rejoice, though now for a little while, if necessary, you have been grieved by various trials, so that the tested genuineness of your faith—more precious than gold that perishes though it is tested by fire—may be found to result in praise and glory and honor at the revelation of Jesus Christ. Though you have not seen him, you love him. Though you do not now see him, you believe in him and rejoice with joy that is inexpressible and filled with glory, obtaining the outcome of your faith, the salvation of your souls.

1 John 3:1–2

See what kind of love the Father has given to us, that we should be called children of God; and so we are. The reason why the world does not know us is that it did not know him. Beloved, we are God's children now, and what we will be has not yet appeared; but we know that when he appears we shall be like him, because we shall see him as he is.

1 John 4:7–11

Beloved, let us love one another, for love is from God, and whoever loves has been born of God and knows God. Anyone who does not love does not know God, because God is love. In this the love of God was made manifest among us, that God sent his only Son into the world, so that we might live through him. In this is love, not that we have loved God but that he loved us and sent his Son to be the propitiation for our sins. Beloved, if God so loved us, we also ought to love one another.

1 John 4:16

So we have come to know and to believe the love that God has for us. God is love, and whoever abides in love abides in God, and God abides in him.

1 John 4:18–19

There is no fear in love, but perfect love casts out fear. For fear has to do with punishment, and whoever fears has not been perfected in love. We love because he first loved us.

63. God's Love for You

John 15:9 (NIV)
"As the Father has loved me, so have I loved you. Now remain in my love."

Psalm 36:5–7 (NIV1984)
Your love, O Lord, reaches to the heavens, your faithfulness to the skies. Your righteousness is like the mighty mountains, your justice like the great deep. O Lord, you preserve both man and beast. How priceless is your unfailing love! Both high and low among men find refuge in the shadow of your wings.

Psalm 103:11–12 (NIV1984)
As high as the heavens are above the earth, so great is His love for those who fear him; as far as the east is from the west, so far has he removed our transgressions from us.

Isaiah 54:10 (NIV)
"Though the mountains be shaken and the hills be removed, yet my unfailing love for you will not be shaken nor my covenant of peace be removed," says the Lord, who has compassion on you.

Ephesians 3:17–19 (NIV1984)
And I pray that you, being rooted and established in love, may have power, together with all the saints, to grasp how wide and long and high and deep is the love of Christ, and to know this love that surpasses knowledge—that you may be filled to the measure of all the fullness of God.

Romans 8:35–39 (NIV)
Who shall separate us from the love of Christ? Shall trouble or hardship or persecution or famine or nakedness or danger or sword? As it is written: "For your sake we face death all day long; we are considered as sheep to be slaughtered." No, in all these things we are more than conquerors through him who loved us. For I am convinced that neither death nor life, neither angels nor demons, neither the present nor the future, nor any powers, neither height nor depth, nor anything else in all creation, will be able to separate us from the love of God that is in Christ Jesus our Lord.

Zephaniah 3:17 (NKJV)
"The Lord your God is in your midst, The Mighty One, will save; He will rejoice over you with gladness; He will quiet you with His love; He will rejoice over you with singing."

Like Love between Husband and Wife

Isaiah 62:5 (NIV)
As a bridegroom rejoices over his bride, so will your God rejoice over you.

Song 2:10–14 (NIV1984)
My lover (picture God here) spoke and said to me, "Arise, my darling, my beautiful one, and come with me. See! The winter is past; the rains are over and gone. Flowers appear on the earth; the season of singing has come, the cooing of doves is heard in our land. The fig tree forms its early fruit; the blossoming vines spread their fragrance. Arise, come, my darling; my beautiful one, come with me."

(Our response) My dove in the clefts of the rock, in the hiding places on the mountainside, show me your face, let me hear your voice; for your voice is sweet, and your face is lovely.

Hosea 2:14–19 (NIV1984)
"Therefore I am now going to allure her; I will lead her into the desert and speak tenderly to her. There I will give her back her vineyards, and will make the Valley of Achor a door of hope. There she will sing as in the days of her youth, as in the day she came up out of Egypt. In that day," declares the Lord, "you will call me 'my husband'; you will no longer call me 'my master.'"

Like Love of a Parent for a Child

Hosea 11:1–4 (NIV1984)
"When Israel was a child, I loved him, and out of Egypt I called my son. But the more I called Israel, the further they went from me. They sacrificed to the Baals and they burned incense to images. It was I who taught Ephraim to walk, taking them by the arms; but they did not realize it was I who healed them. I led them with cords of human kindness, with ties of love; I lifted the yoke from their neck and bent down to feed them."

1 John 3:1 (NIV1984)
How great is the love the Father has lavished on us, that we should be called children of God! And that is what we are![54]

64. "In Christ:" What Does the Bible Say?

If you are ready to spend some time immersed with Jesus exploring the concept of being "In Christ," consider beginning with a study of the following Scriptures.

- Romans 6:1–11
- Galatians 2:20
- Colossians 2:12
- Colossians 3:1
- Romans 5:12–21
- 1 Corinthians 15:21–22
- Romans 5:6–8
- Galatians 1:4
- Galatians 3:13
- 2 Corinthians 5:17

Gaining Perspective

At the moment of our physical birth, we, humankind, are born into Adam's timeline—an "everlasting" timeline with a beginning but no end.

Adam's timeline (everlasting)

In Genesis chapters one and two, we read of the Creation of the world, the beginning of Adam's timeline.

At the Fall (Genesis 3), not only Adam, but all those on his timeline were detoured to hell. The wonderful, glorious news is that upon acceptance of Christ as our personal Lord and Savior, we move out of Adam's timeline (where we are headed to hell) and into Christ's "eternal" timeline—a timeline with no beginning and no end.

Christ's timeline (eternal)

Now hang on and try to wrap your head around this! "In Christ," at the instant of our salvation, we are given both, everlasting and eternal life!! And, wait for it...this will blow your mind:

Eternal Life—Before we had it, we never had it. Once we receive it, we have always had it!

"In Christ:"

Our POSITION *never* changes! We simply cannot step outside of Christ's timeline. Therefore, we are justified, righteous, and sinless.

Our CONDITION, however, changes *constantly*! Our condition is based on our feelings.

Something to Consider:

If we meditate on our condition, it will not (cannot) change our position EVER. If we meditate on our position, it WILL affect our condition. We have a choice! On what will you meditate?

"In Christ" Scriptures for meditation:

- Romans 6:3; Romans 6:5–11
- Romans 6:4
- Colossians 3:1
- Ephesians 2:6
- 2 Timothy 2:12
- Romans 8:17
- Romans 6:14
- Colossians 2:11–12
- Colossians 3:1–3
- John 14:20
- Romans 8:14
- Romans 8:16
- Galatians 2:20
- 2 Corinthians 5:19
- Ephesians 2:8

For further meditation and study:

- What does the passage tell me about my position "in Christ?"
- "In Christ" what do I share with Him?
- What does the Scripture teach me about God?
- What attributes of God are on display?
- Verse Map the verse(s).
- Rewrite the passage in your own words.
- Make connections between the verses.
- Journal your thoughts, insights, and questions.
- Schedule a time of solitude. Spend time with God immersed in these passages.
- Pray the Scriptures.[55]

65. In Christ Jesus

Being "in Christ Jesus" is a stupendous reality. What it means to be in Christ is breathtaking. United to Christ. Bound to Christ. If you are "in Christ" listen to what it means for you:

- In Christ Jesus you were given grace before the world was created. *He gave us grace* **in Christ Jesus** *before the ages began* (2 Timothy 1:9).

- In Christ Jesus you were chosen by God before creation. *[God] chose us* **in [Christ]** *before the foundation of the world* (Ephesians 1:4).

- In Christ Jesus you are loved by God with an inseparable love. *I am sure that neither death nor life, nor angels nor rulers, nor things present nor things to come, nor powers, nor height nor depth, nor anything else in all creation, will be able to separate us from the love of God* **in Christ Jesus our Lord** (Romans 8:38–39).

- In Christ Jesus you were redeemed and forgiven for all your sins. **In [Christ]** we have redemption through his blood, the forgiveness of our trespasses (Ephesians 1:7).

- In Christ Jesus you are justified before God and the righteousness of God in Christ is imputed to you. *For our sake he made him to be sin who knew no sin, so that* **in him** *we might become the righteousness of God* (2 Corinthians 5:21).

- In Christ Jesus you have become a new creation and a son of God. *If anyone is* **in Christ,** *he is a new creation. The old has passed away; behold, the new has come* (2 Corinthians 5:17). **In Christ** *Jesus you are all sons of God, through faith* (Galatians 3:26).

- In Christ Jesus you have been seated in the heavenly places even while He lived on earth. *[God] raised us up with him and seated us with him in the heavenly places* **in Christ Jesus** (Ephesians 2:6).

- In Christ Jesus all the promises of God are Yes for you. 2 Corinthians 1:20, *All God's promises have been fulfilled* **in Christ** *with a resounding "Yes"* (2 Corinthians 1:20, NLT).

- In Christ Jesus you are being sanctified and made holy. *To the church of God that is in Corinth, to those sanctified* **in Christ Jesus** (1 Corinthians 1:2).

- In Christ Jesus everything you really need will be supplied. *My God will supply every need of yours according to his riches in glory* **in Christ Jesus** (Philippians 4:19).

- In Christ Jesus the peace of God will guard your heart and mind. *The peace of God, which surpasses all understanding, will guard your hearts and your minds **in Christ Jesus*** (Philippians 4:7).

- In Christ Jesus you have eternal life. *For the wages of sin is death, but the free gift of God is eternal life **in Christ Jesus our Lord*** (Romans 6:23).

- And in Christ Jesus you will be raised from the dead at the coming of the Lord. *For as in Adam all die, so also **in Christ** shall all be made alive* (1 Corinthians 15:22). All those united to Adam in the first humanity die. All those united to Christ in the new humanity rise to live again.

How do we get into Christ?

At the unconscious and decisive level it is God's sovereign work: *God has united you with Christ Jesus* (1 Corinthians 1:30, NLT).

But at the conscious level of our own action, it is through faith. Christ dwells in our hearts *through faith* (Ephesians 3:17). The life we live in union with His death and life *we live by faith in the Son of God* (Galatians 2:20). We are united in His death and resurrection *through faith* (Colossians 2:12).

This is a wonderful truth. Union with Christ is the ground of everlasting joy, and it is free.[56]

66. My Identity in Jesus

In Christ I am…

- **Accepted** – Romans 8:1; Ephesians 1:6; Psalm 139:1–3
- **Adopted** – Galatians 4:7; John 1:12; Romans 8:15
- **An Ambassador** – 2 Corinthians 5:20
- **Beautiful** – Psalm 139:13–16
- **Blessed** – Romans 8:32; Ephesians 1:3
- **Beloved** – Jeremiah 31:3
- **Bold** – 2 Corinthians 3:12
- **A Bride** – Isaiah 62:5
- **A Child of God** – 1 John 3:1
- **Chosen** – 2 Thessalonians 2:13; Ephesians 1:4
- **Co-Heir with Christ** – Romans 8:17
- **Co-Laborer** – 1 Corinthians 3:9
- **Daughter of the King** – Galatians 3:26
- **Delighted in** – Zephaniah 3:17
- **Delivered from Dark Powers** – Colossians 1:13
- **Elevated to Heavenly Places** – Ephesians 2:6
- **Eternal** – Romans 6:23
- **Favored** – Proverbs 8:35
- **Forgiven** – Psalm 103:12; Colossians 1:13–14; 1 Peter 2:24; Ephesians 1:7
- **Free** – John 8:36; Galatians 5:1
- **Friend** – John 15:15
- **Given Grace** – 1 Timothy 1:9
- **God's Workmanship** – Ephesians 2:10
- **Guarded** – Philippians 4:7
- **Healed by His Stripes** – 1 Peter 2:24
- **Human** – Genesis 1:27

- **Innocent Before Him in Love** – Ephesians 1:4
- **Justified** – Romans 5:1; 2 Corinthians 5:21
- **Kept by the Power of God** – 1 Peter 2:24
- **Loved Unconditionally** – John 3:16; 1 John 4:10; Isaiah 43:3; Romans 8:38–39
- **Masterpiece** – Ephesians 2:10
- **More than a Conquerer** – Romans 8:37
- **Never Alone** – Deuteronomy 31:8
- **New Creation** – 2 Corinthians 5:17
- **Not Condemned** – Romans 8:1
- **One with Him** – 1 Corinthians 6:17
- **Overcoming the World** – 1 John 5:5
- **Predestined to Sonship** – Ephesians 1:5
- **Quickened Together with Christ** – Ephesians 2:5
- **Redeemed** – Ephesians 1:7; Galatians 3:13
- **Righteous** – 2 Corinthians 5:21
- **Saint** – 1 Corinthians 6:11
- **Sanctified** – 1 Corinthians 1:2
- **Sealed** – Ephesians 1:13
- **Seated in the Heavenly Places** – Ephesians 2:6
- **Secure** – Jeremiah 29:11
- **Set Apart** – 1 Peter 2:9
- **Sweet Aroma** – 2 Corinthians 2:15
- **Temple of the Holy Spirit** – 1 Corinthians 6:19
- **To His Praise** – Ephesians 1:12
- **Transformed** – Romans 12:2
- **Unto His Glory** – Ephesians 1:14
- **Victorious** – 1 Corinthians 15:57; Psalm 18:35
- **Washed Clean (Washed in His Blood)** – Isaiah 1:18; Revelation 1:5
- **Whole in Christ** – Colossians 2:10

- **Wonderfully Made** – Psalm 139:14
- **(X)Crucified with Christ** – Galatians 2:20
- **Yoked Together with Believers** – 2 Corinthians 6:14
- **Zealous of Good Works** – Titus 2:14

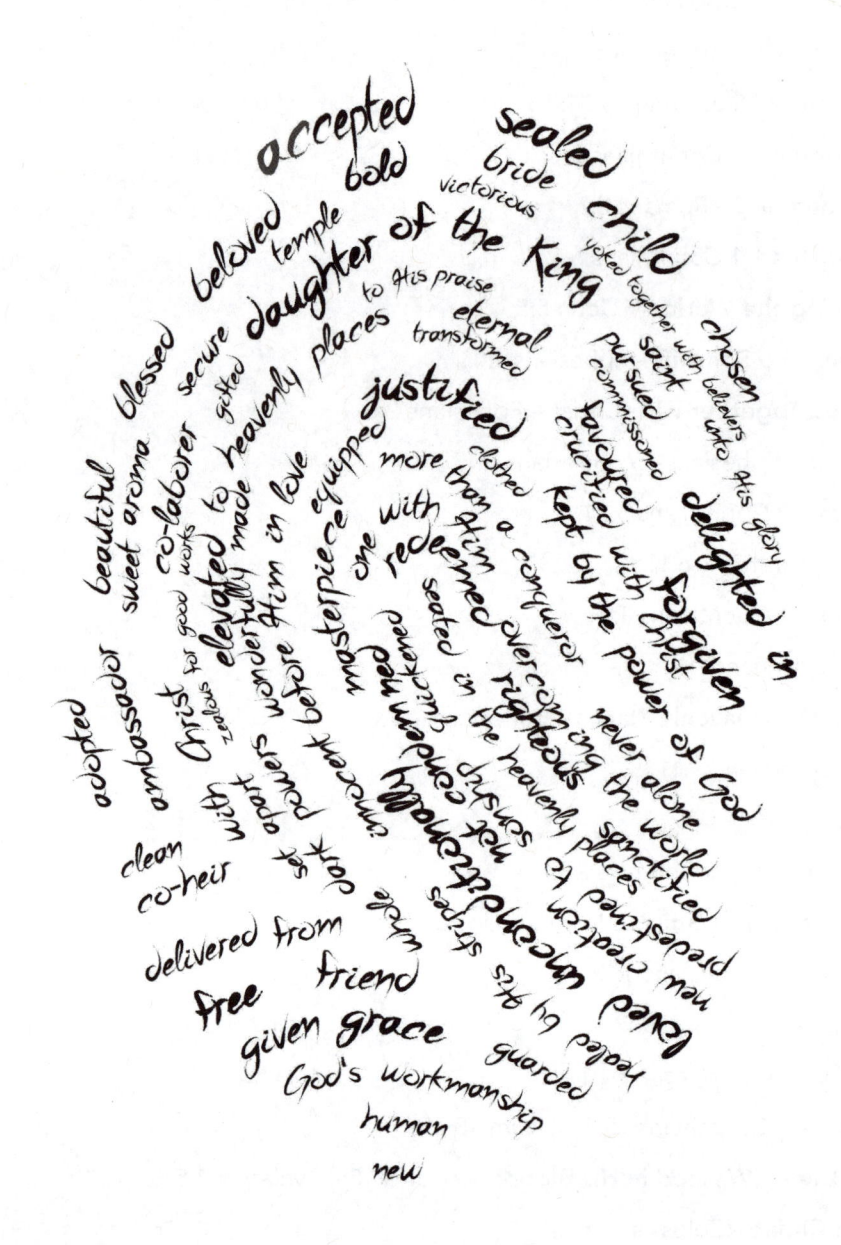

67. Oh, How He Loves Me

- *He has engraved me on the palms of His hands (Isaiah 49:16).*
- *His love for me is as high as the heavens are above the earth (Psalm 103:11).*
- *He delights in me and rejoices over me with singing (Zephaniah 3:17).*
- *He rejoices over me like a bridegroom rejoices over his bride (Isaiah 62:5).*
- *He knows me intimately (Matthew 10:30).*
- *He carries me close (Isaiah 40:11).*
- *He is always with me (Psalm 73:23).*
- *He holds my hand (Psalm 73:23).*
- *He is able to do far more abundantly than all I can ask or imagine (Ephesians 3:20).*
- *He freely forgives me (1 John 1:9).*
- *He created me (Psalm 139:13–14).*
- *He knew me before I was born (Jeremiah 1:5).*
- *He designed me for a special purpose which He prepared before my birth (Ephesians 2:10).*
- *He will fulfill His purpose for me (Philippians 1:6).*
- *He has planned out my days (Psalm 139:16).*
- *He intercedes for me (Hebrews 7:25).*
- *He bears me up (Psalm 68:19).*
- *He will deliver me from harm (Psalm 91:3).*
- *He restores my soul (Psalm 23:3).*
- *He provides refuge (Psalm 91:4).*
- *He will answer me (Psalm 91:15).*
- *He understands (Hebrews 2:17–18).*
- *He gives life to my mortal body (Romans 8:9–11).*
- *He strengthens me (Philippians 4:13).*
- *He teaches me what is best (Isaiah 48:17).*
- *He upholds me (Isaiah 41:10).*
- *He helps me (Isaiah 41:14).*

- He makes my path level (Isaiah 26:7).
- He leads me beside waters of rest (Psalm 23:2).
- He guides me with His counsel (Psalm 73:24).
- He gives me wisdom (James 1:5).
- He keeps record of all my tears (Psalm 56:8).
- He intercedes for me with groanings too deep for words (Romans 8:26).
- He satisfies my hunger and quenches my thirst (John 6:35).
- He gives me abundant life (John 10:10).
- He laid down His life for me (John 10:11).
- He gives me good and perfect gifts (James 1:17).
- He hears my cry and saves me (Psalm 145:19).
- He gives me the desires of my heart (Psalm 37:4).
- He has mercy on me (Psalm 145:9).
- He fills me with joy (Psalm 16:11).
- He gives me drink from the river of His delights (Psalm 36:8).
- He has made me His child (Galatians 3:26).
- He has given me fullness in Christ (Colossians 2:9–10).
- He has qualified me to share in the inheritance of the saints (Colossians 1:12).
- He has given me a glorious inheritance (Ephesians 1:18).
- He raised me up and seated me with Christ in the heavenly places (Ephesians 2:6).
- He lavishes upon me all the riches of His grace (Ephesians 1:8).
- He blots out my transgressions and does not remember my sins (Isaiah 43:25).
- He has compassion on me and casts all my sins into the depths of the sea (Micah 7:19).

68. One Word for One Year

WHAT?

One Word is a single word on which someone chooses to focus every day for an entire year.

WHY?

One Word provides focus for daily living and spiritual growth. To be most effective the chosen word should be one that speaks to an area of needed personal growth or desired heart transformation. Thought should also be given to selecting a word that will help to lead one closer to Jesus Christ.

HOW?

Step 1: Purchase a journal. I typically buy an inexpensive composition book or pull a journal I already own off the shelf. I have perfectionistic tendencies which sometimes paralyze me when it comes to making those first marks on a new page in a new journal. Using an inexpensive composition book moves me beyond the paralyses because I'm not upset if I spill something on it or "mess it up" in some way.

Step 2: Choose your word. Select One Word on which to focus for the entire year. It is a good idea to reflect on the previous year and where you are currently in your spiritual journey. Listen to others. Ask questions. All the while, bathe your choice in prayer.

The possibilities for your word choice are endless. Pay attention. Listen. Gather words. (If you have trouble coming up with a word on your own, consult the list on the following page.)

When your word has been chosen, write it on the cover of your composition book or journal.

Step 3: Over the course of a year, gather your findings. Pray. Ask God to show you what He has to teach you about your word as it relates to your life. Collect everything you can find: quotes, Bible verses, sermon notes, conversation tidbits, graphics, etc. Jot it all down in your journal. (Stay mindful, listening for God's whisperings on the topic as you read scripture, talk with friends & family, listen to sermons, and scroll the internet.)

That is all there is to it. The process is easy, uncomplicated, manageable, and simple; however, it is also meaningful, defining, and transformational.

69. One Word List of Possible Words

One Word that I can focus on every day, all year long. One word that will help me come to better know God, my Father, and lead me closer to Jesus Christ, my Savior.

Abandon	Abide	Abundance
Action	Adapt	Adoration
Adventure	Alive	Ambition
Appreciate	Ask	Awake
Balance	Battle	Be
Believe	Benefits	Blessing
Boldness	Brave	Breathe
Celebrate	Challenge	Change
Choose	Church	Commit
Confidence	Connect	Consistent
Content	Courage	Create
Curious	Dare	Deeper
Determined	Devotion	Different
Diligence	Direction	Discernment
Disciple	Discipline	Discover
Embrace	Empower	Enjoy
Enough	Faith	Faithful
Family	Father	Fearless
Finish	First	Flourish
Focus	Follow	Forgive
Forgiven	Fortitude	Forward

Freedom	Fruitful	Generosity
Gentleness	Go	Goodness
Gospel	Grace	Gratitude
Growth	Healing	Health
Holy	Honor	Hope
Humility	Ignite	Imagine
Integrity	Intention(al)	Invest
Jesus	Joy	Kindness
Kingdom	Lead	Learn
Less	Life	Light
Link	Listen	Live
Love	Mindfulness	Minimize
Momentum	More	New
No	Now	Obedience
Open	Opportunity	Optimism
Organize	Patience	Pause
Peace	Persevere	Persistence
Perspective	Possibility	Power
Pray	Prayer	Presence
Present	Progress	Purity
Purpose	Pursue	Push
Rebuilding	Redemption	Reduce
Reflection	Relationship	Relax
Release	Relentless	Remember

Renewal	Resolve	Rest
Restoration	Restore	Revel
Risk	Sabbath	Sacrifice
Seek	Selah	Self-Control
Serve	Service	Shalom
Shine	Silence	Simplicity
Simplify	Slow	Soar
Soul	Spirit	Stewardship
Stillness	Strength	Surrender
Thrive	Time	Today
Together	Tongue	Transform
Transformation	Transition	Trust
Truth	Unashamed	Unity
Unstoppable	Uplift	Wait
Wholeness	Wisdom	Worship
Write	Yes	Yield

70. Preach the Gospel to Yourself

WHAT?
Preaching the Gospel to ourselves is the daily habit of rehearsing the truths of the gospel. Done each morning and frequently throughout the day, this practice serves to remind us of the importance and power of the Gospel.

This work of Preaching the Gospel to ourselves is both a preemptive and a responsive work. Preemptively, preaching to ourselves feeds our soul, helps to properly fix our focus, and equips us for battle. Responsively, this practice helps to keep us from being mangled and torn when the bumps of life hit…and they will.

WHY?
- We are so easily distracted.
- We are prone to lose focus.
- We need continual reminding that the Gospel is of first importance (1 Corinthians 15:3).
- We are given to making comparisons.
- We are pros at throwing the grandest of pity parties.
- We are commanded to discipline our mind, to take every thought captive in obedience to Christ (2 Corinthians 10:4–5).

HOW?
- In order to effectively preach the gospel to ourselves, our lives must be saturated with the gospel. This means we must keep the gospel front and center.
- Engage with the Gospel (Read it thoughtfully. Memorize it. Study it.)
- Pray Scripture.
- Sing Scripture and the message of the Gospel.
- Read Gospel-focused books.
- Remember. Review how the gospel has affected your life. (Much as Paul did in 1 Timothy 1:12–17.)

Preemptively – Engage in any of these gospel-saturating activities on a daily basis. Begin your day in the gospel and revisit it several times throughout.

Responsively – When disappointments and hard circumstances hit, don't get swallowed up in listening to the unhealthy, destructive self-talk that inevitably ensues. Rather, learn to recognize the unhealthy lies and respond immediately with the truth of the gospel.

- Recognize the lie(s) you are telling yourself.
- STOP!
- Preach the truth of the Gospel to your soul.

71. Scriptures for Preaching the Gospel to Yourself

Preach: The Cross

NEVER STOP CONCENTRATING ON THE WONDERS OF JESUS CRUCIFIED!

1 Corinthians 15:1–3
Now I would remind you, brothers, of the gospel I preached to you, which you received, in which you stand, and by which you are being saved, if you hold fast to the word I preached to you—unless you believed in vain. For I delivered to you as of first importance what I also received: that Christ died for our sins in accordance with the Scriptures.

Isaiah 53:10
Yet it was the will of the Lord to crush him; he has put him to grief; when his soul makes an offering for guilt, he shall see his offspring; he shall prolong his days; the will of the Lord shall prosper in his hand.

Habakkuk 3:18
I will rejoice in the Lord; I will take joy in the God of my salvation.

Matthew 28:6
"He is not here, for he has risen, as he said. Come, see the place where he lay."

Mark 14:32–35
And they went to a place called Gethsemane. And he said to his disciples, "Sit here while I pray." And he took with him Peter and James and John, and began to be greatly distressed and troubled. And he said to them, "My soul is very sorrowful, even to death. Remain here and watch." And going a little farther, he fell on the ground and prayed that, if it were possible, the hour might pass from him.

Luke 22:42
"Father, if you are willing, remove this cup from me. Nevertheless, not my will, but yours, be done."

Romans 3:24–26
[All] are justified by his grace as a gift, through the redemption that is in Christ Jesus, whom God put forward as a propitiation by his blood, to be received by faith. This was to show God's righteousness, because in his divine forbearance he had passed over former sins. It was to show his righteousness at the present time, so that he might be just and the justifier of the one who has faith in Jesus.

Romans 6:11
So you also must consider yourselves dead to sin and alive to God in Christ Jesus.

Preach: Forgiveness

Psalm 103:12
As far as the east is from the west, so far does he remove our transgressions from us.

Psalm 130:3–4
If you, O Lord, should mark iniquities, O Lord, who could stand? But with you there is forgiveness, that you may be feared.

Isaiah 1:18
"Come now, let us reason together, says the Lord: though your sins are like scarlet, they shall be as white as snow; though they are red like crimson, they shall become like wool."

Isaiah 38:17
Behold, it was for my welfare that I had great bitterness; but in love you have delivered my life from the pit of destruction, for you have cast all my sins behind your back.

Isaiah 43:25
"I, I am he who blots out your transgressions for my own sake, and I will not remember your sins."

Isaiah 53:6
All we like sheep have gone astray; we have turned—every one—to his own way; and the Lord has laid on him the iniquity of us all.

Micah 7:19
He will again have compassion on us; he will tread our iniquities underfoot. You will cast all our sins into the depths of the sea.

Romans 4:7–8
"Blessed are those whose lawless deeds are forgiven, and whose sins are covered; blessed is the man against whom the Lord will not count his sin."

Romans 8:1
There is therefore now no condemnation for those who are in Christ Jesus.

Ephesians 1:7
In him we have redemption through his blood, the forgiveness of our trespasses, according to the riches of his grace.

Colossians 2:13–14
And you, who were dead in your trespasses and the uncircumcision of your flesh, God made alive together with him, having forgiven us all our trespasses, by canceling the record of debt that stood against us with its legal demands. This he set aside, nailing it to the cross.

Hebrews 8:12
"For I will be merciful toward their iniquities, and I will remember their sins no more."

Hebrews 10:17–18
"I will remember their sins and their lawless deeds no more." Where there is forgiveness of these, there is no longer any offering for sin.

72. The Spiritual Practice of Walking

It is there over and over again in the pages of His Word, the invitation to walk with Jesus. We can walk with Him in prayer, in gratitude, in humility, in the reading of the Bible, and in so many other ways. But maybe, just maybe from time to time, we should simply take the invitation literally.

Ways to Walk with Jesus

- Slow down. See if you can walk without needing to get anywhere in particular or in a certain amount of time.

- Pray as you walk.

- Notice your surroundings and thank God for each thing that catches your eye.

- Meditate on a verse or passage of Scripture. Think through the details and your questions about the passage. Turn it over in your mind.

- Be present with God.

- Listen. Don't talk. What is God speaking to you right now?

- Practice Preaching to Yourself.

- Reflect on your day, on your relationship with God, on your spiritual growth.

- Breathe periodic breath prayers.

- Praise His attributes—A through Z.

- Quote your Scripture memory work.

Journaling

SOUL NOURISHMENT RESOURCES

73. The Benefits of Journaling

- Helps us build an authentic relationship with God.
- Provides a great barometric reading of our heart.
- Becomes a record of our life.
- Explores our true self.
- Exposes our anxiety.
- Cultivates deeper understandings.
- Facilitates learning: about ourselves, our relationships, our life situations.
- Provides clarity.
- Organizes our thoughts.
- Brings out thoughts that might never have occurred otherwise.
- Makes connections regarding events in our lives.
- Affords an opportunity to play with ideas.
- Helps make our thoughts and prayers more concrete.
- Records spiritual thoughts and realizations.
- Helps us focus on the topic and on speaking to God.
- Forces us to take time on a regular basis to sit with God and make some sense of life.
- Assists us in keeping a balance between head and heart.
- Makes a record of our spiritual growth, much like the growth charts of children.
- Marks out a time for us to listen as God speaks wisdom to our lives.
- Clarifies our understanding of the nature and will of God.
- Facilitates connections: to God, to ourselves, and to others as we ask probing questions, think through issues, and put the "stuff" tumbling around in our heads on paper.
- Helps us to slow down and enjoy the "being" side of life.

- Relaxes us.

- Provides a sense of planned "margin" in our full days.

- Helps us simplify and view what is, instead of what isn't.

- Assists us in taking stock of the present.

- Offers a safe place to observe, understand, and then move toward change.

74. Some Journaling Ideas

- Look back.
- Write about fun moments.
- Pray on paper.
- Jot down what you're learning lately (insights, wisdom, mistakes).
- Work through decisions.
- Record quotes or stories you want to remember.
- Note your observations about how life works.
- Hang on to precious moments.
- Record scenes you want to keep with you.
- List ideas or goals for the future.
- Document your values.
- Write mission statements.
- Reflect on notes from sermons or lectures.
- Compose a letter to someone.
- Dig into Scripture.
- Honestly answer questions for the purpose of soul-searching and self-reflection.
- Record thoughts and memories to be passed on to your children or grandchildren.

75. Questions to Use When Journaling

Ever feel like you just can't find the answer? Often, we do not have answers because we have not asked the right questions. Questions help us see potential solutions, ones that lie just below the surface. Your journal is a safe place for posing great questions and seeking answers.

1. Why do I keep doing this?
2. How's that working for me?
3. What do I need?
4. What am I willing to do next?
5. What is my next step?
6. What obstacles do I anticipate? How will I overcome them?
7. What needs to be in place for this to happen?
8. What resources do I need?
9. What do I need in order to succeed?
10. Why do I feel so numb? Out of control? Hurt? Angry? Selfish?
11. How do my actions reveal what I truly believe?
12. How can I tangibly express my love to _____?
13. How can I help without trying to fix?
14. Why am I getting so involved in this?
15. What am I afraid of?
16. What's the worst that can happen?
17. If that happens, so what?
18. Where do I see myself in 5 years? 10 years? 25 years?
19. How does that hold up next to Scripture?
20. Is it truth?

21. Where do I experience God in my life?

22. Is Jesus my ultimate purpose in life?

23. What am I longing for in my relationship with God?

24. Am I being filled daily with God's love? God's peace? God's joy?

25. Who am I longing to *be*? (Not what am I longing to do?)

26. What am I thankful for?

27. What do I feel sorry about?

28. What are my struggles?

29. What is causing me to feel stress?

30. What is my current situation?

31. What is right with my life?

76. Scripture Journaling

Scripture Journaling is a way of studying and responding to the Bible with your own words, sketches, stenciling, images, painting, stamping, or other art media.

What You Need:
- Journaling Bible
- Blank journal, art book, or composition book
- Pencil
- Fine tip black ink pen
- Eraser
- *Optional:* colored pencils, colored markers, Crayola Twistables, stickers, stamps and stamp pads, washi tape, water colors, micron pens, scrap paper, baby wipes, any art materials you have on hand

Process:

Step 1: Gather your materials. Consider turning on some music to listen to as you journal.

Step 2: Choose a Scripture verse or passage to journal. (Your selection can come from anywhere: a current Bible study, your personal devotions, family Bible reading, sermon notes, song lyrics, an internet search. The possibilities are endless.)

Step 3: Read your verse thoughtfully. Ponder how you want to journal the verse:
- Using words only
- Writing out the verse word for word
- Recording your thoughts about the verse
- Combining stickers with words
- Sketching or drawing
- Using song lyrics

Step 4: Date your entry.

Step 5: Have fun journaling your Scripture. Don't forget to continue meditating on your Scripture as you work.

Keep in mind that there is absolutely no right or wrong way to Scripture journal. You cannot do it the wrong way! The idea behind Scripture Journaling is NOT that you create great art. In fact, you do not even have to include art. The idea is that you **connect with God and His Word.**

Note: If you are working in a Journaling Bible, be careful not to use materials that will bleed through your pages. You can test your materials on a blank page in the back of your Bible.

77. Topical Scripture Journaling

Most Scripture journaling methods call for your journal to be organized by book, chapter, passage, or verse of the Bible. Topical Scripture Journaling is different in that your journal will be organized by topic.

A bit of effort is required in the initial set-up of a Topical Scripture Journal, but once it's ready to go, this type of journal provides a wonderful place in which to collect everything you find regarding your chosen Bible topics.

What You Need:

- Blank journal or composition book
- Pen or pencil
- Optional: divider tabs, markers and embellishments for decorating

Set-up Process:

Step 1: Number all of the pages in your journal. Be sure to number them front and back.

Step 2: Write down the total number of pages in your journal. (Example: Page numbering stops at page 162. Write down 162. This may help you in deciding how many pages to allot per topic.)

Step 3: Write "Table of Contents" on the top of the first two pages.

Step 4: If you want to fill your topics in *before* you begin journaling, go ahead and write them in on your "Table of Contents." (You choose whether you want them in alphabetical order or grouped by a category. You also decide how many pages to allot for each topic. This portion of the set-up is entirely up to you. Don't worry about whether you are leaving enough room for your topics. When a topic's pages run out, simply write "Go to page #__" at the bottom of the filled-up section and continue the topic on another page in your journal. Lastly, don't forget to write the topic next to the corresponding page number in your "Table of Contents.")

If, however, you make the choice to write your topics in *as you go*, just remember each time you begin a new topic to add it to your "Table of Contents."

Step 5: Write the topic of each page at the top of its assigned page.

Step 6: *OPTIONAL* – Decorate your covers inside and out.

JOURNALING Soul Nourishment Resources

Process for Using Your Topical Scripture Journal:

Step 1: Topics can be added to your journal at any time. When deciding on topics think about:

- What is important to you in your current season of life?
- What words seem to be popping up everywhere you turn?
- What interests you?
- Spend a few days listening.
- Look at your Pinterest pins.

Step 2: Dig into your topic(s) and add to your pages. There are no rules or limits to what can be added. Consider:

- Definitions
- A list of written out Scriptures
- Scriptures written in your own words
- Quotes on the topic
- Your personal thoughts
- Insights you have gained
- Sermon notes
- Programs from conferences & workshops
- Excerpts from books written by Christian authors
- Blog posts
- Anything you can put in a book

Absolutely anything can be put into your Topical Scripture Journal so think outside the box—include sketches, diagrams, poems, artwork, scrapbooking, or anything you enjoy!

Note: Remember, when it comes to methods of engaging with Scripture and journaling, There are NO rules! Your Topical Scripture Journal does NOT even have to be TOPICAL. Try setting one up by book of the Bible or by chapter!

78. Possible Topics for Topical Scripture Journaling

Advent	Accountability	Attributes of God
Blessing	Christian Living	Christmas
Courage	Covenant(s)	Creation
Doctrines	Easter	Faith
The Fall	Family	Forgiveness
Friendship	Fruit of the Spirit	God the Father
The Gospel	Gratitude	Holy Spirit
Home	Honesty	Humility
Identity in Christ	Integrity	Jesus Christ
Joy	Knowledge	Love
Marriage	Modesty	Motherhood
Obedience	Patriarchal Blessings	Physical Health
Plan of Salvation	Prayer	Resurrection
The Sabbath	Scripture	The Second Coming
Service	Sexual Purity	Silence
Solitude	Sovereignty	Spiritual Disciplines
Temptation	Testimony	Truth
Virtue	Wisdom	The Word of God

79. Whole-Brain Journaling Techniques

Imagery: Using God's Gift of Imagination to Integrate Truth

God uses powerful imagery throughout Scripture to open not only our minds but our hearts to truth. His imagery often uses descriptive words and metaphors to engage us at a soul level with spiritual lessons for our lives.

Likewise, we can engage our God-given ability to visualize stories or verses, activating whole-brain learning, in order to integrate the truth more effectively.

Example:
Enter his gates with thanksgiving, and *his* courts with praise! *Give thanks to him; bless his name!* (Psalm 100:4).

- Engage in a prayerful posture internally by picturing what it is like to walk into the gates of The Great Almighty One.

- Then, as though you are taking one thoughtful step at a time into the courts of the King, approach His throne (called the Throne of Grace). Picture the courts with luxurious curtains, huge ceilings, and rich marble floors.

- As you enter, hear Him welcome you and invite you to come closer. Tell Him what is on your mind and heart.

Spiritual Journaling in Nature

The Lord tells us in Romans chapter 1 verse 20 (NASB), *For since the creation of the world His invisible attributes, His eternal power and divine nature, have been clearly seen, being understood through what has been made, so they are without excuse.* His attributes, wisdom, and glory are all around us when we step outside. Creation, chemistry, physics, biology, etc. all point directly to a Supreme, vastly intelligent Creator. Proverbs tells of Wisdom being at His side as he created all that is. Wisdom is seen and observed throughout nature.

- Go outside with a blank journal and pen, and perhaps a few colored pencils.

- Get comfortable and close your eyes.

- Take 5 long slow breaths in, exhaling more slowly than you inhale. (Don't skip this, please!) This activates your parasympathetic system, relaxing your body at a physical, fundamental level.

- Next, notice what you feel on your skin. A breeze? The temperature? Pause, notice a few more things you feel.

- Notice what you smell. Go slowly, pause to see if there is anything else.

- Notice what you hear. What else?

- Go through all your senses, focusing slowly. Pause and see if there is anything else.

- Lastly, open your eyes and notice what you see. Allow yourself to slow down to simply notice what strikes you. It may be big or small, light or dark, complex, or simple and humble.

- Jot a few notes—words and phrases to capture this moment.

- Now draw a simple picture of what one thing captures your attention the most.

- Journal about what this means to you. What about it drew you?

- Write a Haiku, based on the words and phrases you jotted down in the experience of mindfulness above. A Haiku is a three line poem, with 5 syllables in the first line, 7 syllables in the second, and 5 syllables in the third line. It does not need to rhyme. It doesn't need to be beautiful. It simply needs to express the essence of the moment you noticed.[57]

80. Create

Sometimes when we pray there seem to be no words. Romans 8:26 says, *Likewise the Spirit helps us in our weakness. For we do not know what to pray for as we ought, but the Spirit himself intercedes for us with groanings too deep for words.* This not only happens when we pray. There can be other times when we desire to connect with God that we simply do not have words.

Creative expression can enable us to connect with God beyond words. The process of creating allows for clearing of the mind and helps to make space for God's presence. Creative expression can be a "place" where the veil between heaven and earth seems more transparent.

A Toolbox of Creative Expression

Art Journaling
Art Journaling involves using color, words, and images as a means of personal expression or prayer. Create an art journal of praise to your Heavenly Father, a prayer art journal to record your prayers, or a Scripture art journal as you meditate and reflect upon Scripture. For something a little different, try art journaling sermon notes or song lyrics.

Collages
As a response to Scripture, or as you enter your time of prayer, tear paper and then use glue to create a visual representation. As you tear the paper, be aware of your brokenness and the parts of life that need healing, wholeness, and restoration. Surrender the brokenness. Then begin to make a new creation out of the broken pieces. Your collage can be an abstract work. Allow the colors to reflect your mood and where you are spiritually. If color papers and abstracts aren't your thing, create a collage with words, pictures, and/or Bible verses and make them around a theme or topic.

Soulbooking
Love scrapbooking? Give your favorite hobby a soul-lift by incorporating your faith into your scrapbooks. Choose your favorite Scriptures, things you are learning, biblical topics, and scrapbook them. As an added bonus the process of creating your scrapbook will itself provide opportunity for deep reflection and meaningful time with God.

Home Décor
Bring your faith into your home décor. Craft wall crosses, Scripture plaques, art canvases, posters and more to display in your home. This is an artistic way to display your faith as a reminder and encouragement to you and your family and a lovely way to share your faith with visitors to your home.

"Joy Journey" Notes

Create "joyful" reminders. Use cardstock, paint, paper-stitching, rubber stamping, encouraging words, and any other art materials you enjoy, to create little "joy" cards. Give your creations to others as a means of encouragement, and don't forget to keep a few to place around your home or in your car.

Scripture Canvas for the Soul

Use your favorite mixed media or art technique to design a Scripture canvas for your wall. Use Bible verses and/or inspirational quotes to create a "truth statement" about who you are down to the core. Or use Bible verses, names of God, and attributes of God to create a "wonderstruck" piece.

Vision Boards/Dream Boards/Vision Maps

Using Scripture, inspiring quotes, words, and images, create a vision board. Items can simply be drawn onto a poster board, cut from magazines and other sources, or produced using word processing and/or photo editing software. Spend some time alone with God as you plan out your board and then again during the process. This is another wonderful creative activity for self-reflection and for communication with God.

"Words that Mean Something" Art Piece

Love words? Craft beautiful pages using your favorite art media. Hang your pages on the wall or place them in a book. Fill the pages with much-loved words of wisdom such as uplifting Scriptures or inspiring quotes.

As you close this book and begin your journey,

Open God's Love Letter to You!

Dear Friend,

I love you! (John 3:16). I created you in my image (Genesis 1:27) and I called you "very good" (Genesis 1:31). I knit you together in your mother's womb (Psalm 139:13). I know the number of the hairs on your head (Matthew 10:30), and I am familiar with all your ways (Psalm 139:3). My precious thoughts of you are as countless as the sand on the seashore (Psalm 139:17–18).

I am Love (1 John 4:16) and the greatest commandment that I have for you is that you love (Matthew 22:37–40). My love is made complete in you when you receive my love, love me, and love others (1 John 4:7–21). To show you how to live this life of love I've given you Ten Commandments (Exodus 20:1–17), laws that honor me and are good and pleasing to you (Psalm 119).

But you were born in sin, separated from my love (Psalm 51:5), and though you've tried to be good you've missed the mark of my holiness (1 John 1:8). You've hurt others and you've hurt yourself (Romans 2:9). Most of all, your sins are against me (Psalm 51:4). You've hurt me (Luke 19:41) and angered me (Romans 2:8). I am the Lord (Exodus 6:2), the King of Kings (1 Timothy 6:15), and the Righteous Judge (1 Peter 4:5) and it is a terrible thing to come under my judgment (Hebrews 10:31).

To fear me is the beginning of wisdom (Proverbs 1:7). But you don't need to remain afraid of me; if you rely on me then my perfect love will remove all of your fear (1 John 4:18). I am a compassionate and gracious God, slow to anger and abounding in love and faithfulness (Exodus 34:6).

Now, in the person of Jesus Christ, I knock on the door of your heart, waiting for you to let me in (Revelation 3:20). Open the door and I will forgive your sins (Acts 10:43) and choose not to remember them anymore (Isaiah 43:25). I will teach you how to live your daily life with me in the kingdom of the heavens (Matthew 4:17). I will adopt you into my family (Ephesians 1:5) and lavish on you my fatherly love (1 John 3:1). Then you will marvel that I chose you to be my child (Ephesians 1:11–12) and I drew you to myself (John 6:44).

You see I've loved you from the beginning, long before you loved me (1 John 4:19). I sent my son Jesus, the exact representation of my being (Hebrews 1:3), to die on the cross in your place (Romans 5:8), to take upon Himself the punishment that you deserved (Isaiah 53:5), and to take away your sin (John 1:29). For you the mighty Lion sacrificed his life as an innocent Lamb (Revelation 5:5–6). So, you can see that in Jesus I, your Lord and Master, have come to serve you! (John 13:13–14).

When you are "born again" by my Holy Spirit (John 3:3) then you become a new person (2 Corinthians 5:17) with a new heart (Ezekiel 36:26), a new self (Ephesians 4:24), and a new life (Romans 6:4). You have my precious righteousness as a gift (Romans 5:19). Your body becomes a temple for my Holy Spirit (1 Corinthians 6:19), and you become a saint (Ephesians 1:18).

Indeed, I will make your righteousness to shine like the dawn (Psalm 37:6). You will be a crown of glory in my hand (Isaiah 62:3), reflecting my likeness with ever-increasing glory (2 Corinthians 4:18). I am faithful to help you to be holy (1 Thessalonians 5:24) and to complete the good work I've started in you (Philippians 1:6).

So, stand firm in my grace (Galatians 5:1) and fight the good fight of faith (1 Timothy 6:12). When you are tempted to sin, look for the way out that I provide (1 Corinthians 10:13). Resist the devil and submit to me (James 4:7); turn away from sin and toward the good that I provide (Romans 12:21). And when you fail remember that I am waiting for you with open arms, quick to forgive you and to give you another chance (Luke 15:11–31). Satan will accuse you, but call out to Jesus and I will defend you and enable you to overcome him (Revelation 12:10–11). I will rescue your true self from sin (Romans 7:14-25) and condemnation (Romans 8:1).

Remember that the pleasures of sin are fleeting (Hebrews 11:25) and if you find your delight in me instead then you will see that I give you the desires of your heart (Psalm 37:4)—eternal pleasures even! (Psalm 16:11)—and I do far more for you than you can imagine (Ephesians 3:20). Whatever you need, look to me and I will provide it (Philippians 4:19). I will give you love, joy, peace, and all the fruit of my Spirit to fill your soul and to share with others (Galatians 5:22–23).

Since I care so much for you don't worry about getting your needs met and don't worry about tomorrow (Matthew 6:25–34). Just as I look after the little sparrow I will also look after you (Matthew 10:26–31). So give your burdens to me and let me give you rest (Matthew 11:28). Talk to me when you're anxious and let me put you at peace (Philippians 4:6).

No matter what happens, your soul will be safe in my hands (John 10:28). Like a mother bird I'll cover you with my feathers in my nest (Psalm 91:1–4). When rivers of difficulty roar, you will not be swept away. When fiery trials blaze, you will not be burned (Isaiah 43:2). When war breaks out, I will be your fortress, an ever-present help in trouble (Psalm 46). Even when you face death I will take you by the hand and lead you on the joyful path to eternal life (Psalm 16:9–11).

So, don't be afraid when you walk through the valley of the shadow of death because I am your Good Shepherd, and I will be with you, comforting you and protecting you on your journey (Psalm 23), and I will never leave you (Hebrews 13:5).

When enemies come against you I will fight for you (Psalm 44:7). Even when you do what is right people will insult you, criticize you, and mistreat you, but I will bless you (Matthew 5:11). Even when you trust your father and mother they may forsake you, but I will receive you (Psalm 27:10). So if you find yourself poor, remember that I've blessed you with true riches (Luke 6:20). And if you find yourself last in line, remember that with me those who are last will be first (Matthew 20:16). Yes, I will raise you up and exalt you when you are humble before me (Matthew 23:12).

When you are brokenhearted I will draw close to you (Psalm 34:18) and cry with you (John 11:35). I'll collect all your tears in my bottle and record each one in my book (Psalm 56:8). Like a shepherd holding his lamb, I'll carry you close to my heart (Isaiah 40:11). I'll comfort you in your time of sadness (Matthew 5:4), turning your mourning into gladness (Jeremiah 31:13) and your weakness into strength (2 Corinthians 12:9–10). I will put a happy new song in your mouth (Psalm 40:3) and give you a beautiful new name (Isaiah 62:2).

Even the difficulty and pain you experience can be to your benefit if you endure these hardships as loving discipline from me, opportunities for you to be trained in the ways of righteousness and peace (Hebrews 12:6–11). Always remember that when you love me and seek my purposes, all things will work together for your good (Romans 8:28).

I am for you and not against you (Romans 8:31). If I have been misrepresented to you by religious people who claim to know me but don't (John 8:41-44), then know that I am against those hypocrites (Matthew 23). And if your earthly father has not shown you my fatherly love, then please realize that I offer you more than he ever could (Matthew 7:9–11). I am the perfect Father (Matthew 5:48), the Father from whom all true fatherhood derives its name (Ephesians 3:15), and I love to give you good gifts (Matthew 7:11).

With me on your side your future is bright and full of hope! My plans are to prosper you and not to harm you (Jeremiah 29:11), to give you abundant life (John 10:10) now and forever (John 3:36). Call to me and I will answer you (Jeremiah 33:3); listen and you will hear my voice directing you (Isaiah 30:21); tune into your heart and you will sense my instructions (Psalm 16:7). My Holy Spirit will be your Counselor (John 14:15, 26; 16:7). Don't walk alone; walk in my Spirit (Galatians 5:25), trust in me, and I will direct your path (Proverbs 3:4-5) and bless you wonderfully (Ephesians 1:3).

I have gifted you to serve me in my kingdom (Matthew 25:14-23) and I want to make you great (Psalm 18:35). So discover your gift and use it in the body of Christ (Romans 12:4-8). I have important work for you to do, work that I will help you to accomplish by working alongside you (Haggai 2:4). Together we can accomplish great dreams (Mark 10:27) and move mountains! (Matthew 17:20).

You are the light of the world, so shine my light to those who are lost (Matthew 5:14). Show your love for me by loving those who are in need (1 John 3:17–18). You serve me when you feed the hungry, provide shelter for the homeless, clothe the poor, care for the sick, and visit those in prison (Matthew 25:34–40). And always be prepared to talk to the hopeless in a respectful way about the good news of my grace demonstrated in Jesus (1 Peter 3:15). Do these things for people from every nation and every language, training them to follow Jesus (Matthew 28:19–20).

But you're not just my servant: you're my friend! (John 15:15). More than that you're my beloved child (1 John 3:1). You're precious and honored in my sight (Isaiah 43:4) and I rejoice over you with singing (Zephaniah 3:17).

I delight in you like a bridegroom for his bride (Isaiah 62:5). I will always love you (Jeremiah 31:3) and nothing can ever change that! (Romans 8:38–39). **One day soon in Jesus I will return** to bring you and all my followers to the heavenly home that I have prepared for you (John 14:2). I will wipe away your tears and take away your pain forever (Revelation 21:3–4), and I will reward you for all the good that you've done in my name (Revelation 22:12). Heaven will be more beautiful and wonderful than you can imagine (Revelation 21:10–27). There we will sing to God with angels (Revelation 7:9–17), feast at banquets (Matthew 22:14), and rule over cities (Luke 19:11–26).

Love,

God

P.S. If it's hard for you to trust my words and to receive my love in your heart then I urge you to work through this with one of my ambassadors (2 Corinthians 5:20) and to get involved in a caring community in the body of Christ where you can grow into my love (Romans 12:5).[58]

For Further Reading

Thomas à Kempis, *The Imitation of Christ*. Many editions available. Apart from the Bible itself, this is undoubtedly the most republished work in Christian history. Absolutely indispensable.

Richard Baxter, *The Practical Works of Richard Baxter*. Grand Rapids: Baker Book House, 1981.

Louis Bouyer, *A History of Christian Spirituality*. 3 volumes. New York: Seabury Press, 1982.

Francis De Sales, *Introduction to the Devout Life*. Garden City, N.Y.: Doubleday, 1957.

Charles Finney, *Revival Lectures*. Old Tappan, N.J.: Fleming H. Revell Company, n.d.

John Flavel, *Keeping Your Heart*. ReadaClassic.com, 2010.

Richard Foster, *Celebration of Discipline: The Path to Spiritual Growth*. Harper San Francisco; 3rd edition, 1998.

William Law, *A Serious Call to a Devout and Holy Life*. New York: Paulist Press, 1978—and many other editions.

Andrew Murray, *Especially Humility* and *Absolute Surrender*. Many editions.

Henri Nouwen, *The Way of the Heart*. New York: Ballantine Books, 1981.

A. W. Tozer, *The Pursuit of God*. Harrisburg, PA: Christian Publications, Inc, 1948.

Dallas Willard, *The Spirit of the Disciplines: Understanding How God Changes Lives*. HarperOne, 1999.

Octavius Winslow, *Personal Declension and Revival of Religion in the Soul*. TheClassics.us, 2013.

NOTES

1. Dallas Willard, taken from *The Great Omission*, Copyright © 2014 by Dallas Willard. (Grand Rapids, MI: Used by permission of HarperOne, www.harperone.com, 2009), 122–123.

2. John Ortberg, taken from *Soul Keeping: Caring for the Most Important Part of You*, Copyright © 2014 by John Ortberg. (Grand Rapids, MI Used by permission of Zondervan, www.zondervan.com). [Accessed by video, no page numbers.]

3. Dallas Willard. *Renovation of the Heart*. Copyright © 2002. (Nashville, TN: Used by permission of NavPress. All rights reserved. Represented by Tyndale House Publishers, Inc.) (This product is available for purchase at www.tyndaledirect.com), 54.

4. Willard, 318.

5. Kathy Butryn, taken from "Journal Your Devotions - Discover How Cultivating Essential Spiritual Habits Can Transform Your Daily Quiet Time" 23 April 2018. [Accessed online, no page numbers.]

6. John Flavel, taken from *Keeping the Heart*, (Christian Heritage, 2012), 4.

7. Margaret Feinberg, *Wonderstruck*, © 2012, (Franklin, TN: Worthy Publishing, a division of Worthy Media, Inc., www.worthypublishing.com), 5.

8. Ortberg, *Soul Keeping*, 89.

9. Feinberg, *Wonderstruck*, 4.

10. Ortberg, 90.

11. A. W. Tozer, taken from *The Pursuit of God*, (Bloomington, MN:Bethany House Publishers, 2013), 12–13.

12. Shawn Young, taken from "How to Care for Your Soul", (InterVarsity Christian Fellowship/USA.) [Accessed online, no page numbers.]

13. Willard, *Great Omission*, 52.

14. Dallas Willard, taken from *The Spirit of the Disciplines*, Copyright © 1999 by Dallas Willard. (Grand Rapids, MI: Used by permission of HarperOne. www.harperone.com), 252.

15. Oswald Chambers, taken from *Christian Disciplines*, © 1936 by the Oswald Chambers Publications Association, Ltd. (Grand Rapids, MI: Used by permission of Discovery House Publishers). All rights reserved. [Wording provided by Discovery House.] 151–152.

16. Alan Fadling, taken from *An Unhurried Life: Following Jesus' Rhythms of Work and Rest,* (, Downers, Grove, IL: IVP Books, 2013), 164.

17. Willard, *Spirit*, 226–227.

18. Madeline L'engle, *Walking on Water: Reflections on Faith and Art*, (Convergent Books part of Penguin/Random House), [ebook version], 201.

19. Feinberg, *Wonderstruck*, 92.

20. Larry Crabb, taken from , (Nashville, TN: Nelson, 1997, www.thomasnelson.com), 5.

21. Henri Nouwen, taken from *Intimacy*, Copyright © 1969 by Henri Nouwen. Used by permission of (Grand Rapids, MI: HarperOne. www.harperone.com), 201.

22. Dr. Henry Cloud, Dr. John Townsend, taken from *Safe People: How to Find Relationships That Are Good for You and Avoid Those That Aren't*, Copyright © 1996 by Dr. Henry Cloud and Dr. John Townsend. (Grand Rapids, MI: Zondervan), www.zondervan.com, 143.

23. Henry Blackaby, and Richard and Claude King *Experiencing God: Knowing and Doing the Will of God*, (Nashville, TN: Life Way Press, 2007) Reprinted and used by permission, 55.

24. Nicole Whitacre, "Maybe This Year," http://www.girltalkhome.com/blog/maybe-this-year/, 03 January 2012.

25. Willard, *Great Ommission*, 125.

26. Bro. Lawrence, taken from *The Practice of the Presence of God*. (Booklassic, 2015), 38.

27. Dictionary.com http://www.dictionary.com/browse/thanksgiving, Copied and pasted information from the red CITE button on dictionary.com

28. Thomas Watson, *All Things for Good* (Carlisle, PA: The Banner of Truth Trust, 1986), 74.

29. Warren Wiersbe, taken from *Real Worship: Playground, Battleground, or Holy Ground?* © 2000. (Ada, MI: Baker Books. www.bakerpublishinggroup.com, 2000), 31.

30. Mindy Caligure, *Discovering Soul Care*, (Downers Grove, IL: InterVarsity Press, 2007), 13–20.

31. Charissa Jaeger-Sanders, taken from *Sacred Space*, (www.graceworksstudio.org/).

32. Asheritah Ciuciu, taken from *The Ultimate Guide to Connect with God*, (https://onethingalone.com/ultimate-list-creative-ways-connect-god-120-ideas/).

33. Ben Griffin, "How to Pray: A Biblical Guide to Prayer Infographic," Jesus Rhythm, (http://www.jesus-rhythm.com/prayerguide/#), 27 February 2014, Web 20 March 2018. Blog URL.

34. John Piper, © Desiring God Foundation. Source: desiringGod.org, (https://www.desiringgod.org/articles/9-ways-to-pray-for-your-soul).

35. Sybil MacBeth, *Praying in Color: Drawing a New Path to God*, (Brewster, MA: Paraclete Press:, 2013), 19-20, 29-38.

36. MacBeth, *Praying*.

37. Maurice Roberts, The Thought of God, (Carlisle, PA: Banner of Truth, 1994).

38. Kari Denker, "Simple Bible Meditation for Complete Beginners," (http://www.stonesoupforfive.com/2015/06/simple-bible-meditation-for-beginners.html). Blog URL

39. Donald Whitney, *Spiritual Disciplines for the Christian Life*, (Colorado Springs, CO: NavPress, 2014), 68.

40. Chuck Swindoll, taken from *Growing Strong in the Seasons of Life*, ©1994 by Chuck Swindoll, (Grand Rapids, MI: Zondervan, www.zondervan.com), 53.

41. Dallas Willard, taken from "Spiritual Formation in Christ for the Whole Life and Whole Person," (*Vocatio*, Vol. 12, No. 2, Spring, 2001), 7.

42. Arabah Joy, taken from *50 Most Important Scriptures to Memorize*, (https://arabahjoy.com/50-most-important-scriptures-to-memorize).

43. Alan Fadling, taken from *An Unhurried Life: Following Jesus' Rhythms of Work and Rest*, (Downers, Grove, IL: InterVarsity Press Books, 2013), 168–170.

44. Donald Whitney, taken from "31 Questions to Ask for a More Christ-Centered 2018," by Donald Whitney (http://equip.sbts.edu/article/31-questions-ask-christ-centered-2018/), 24 March 2018. Blog URL

45. Mindy Caliguire, taken from *Spiritual Friendship*, (Downers Grove, IL: InterVarsity Press, 2007), 42–45.

46. Tim Lane and Paul Tripp, taken from *Relationships: A Mess Worth Making*, (Greensboro, NC: New Growth Press, 2006), 113–115.

47. Rachel Wojnarowski, Taken from "20 Things to Say to Encourage a Friend", (http://rachelwojo.com/things-to-say-to-encourage-a-friend/), April 17, 2018. Blog URL.

48. Marjorie J. Thompson, taken from *Soul Feast: An Invitation to the Christian Spiritual Life*, (Westminster John Knox Press, Louisville, KY, 1995), 83.

49. Charles F. Stanley, *Life Principles Bible, eBook*, Copyright © 2013 by Charles Stanley. (Nashville, TN: Thomas Nelson. www.thomasnelson.com), 582.

50. David Mathis, © Desiring God Foundation, Source: desiringGod.org, (https://www.desiringgog.org/articles/fasting-for-beginners), Blog URL.

51. Bill Gaultiere, taken from "Hungry Hearts Scriptures", (http://www.soulshepherding.org/2006/07/hungry-heart-scriptures/), 02/April 2018. Blog URL.

52. Arthur W. Pink, taken from *The Attributes of God*, (Grand Rapids, MI: Baker Books, 2003), This resource was put together (loosely) from the chapter titles of this book. Chapters begin on pages 9, 15, 21, 27, 35, 40, 47, 52, 59, 68, 75, 81, 87, 94, 101, 108, 116.

53. Unlocking the Bible, "My Father, (https://www.pinterest.com/pin/415175659376205627/).

54. Bill Craig, "God's Love for You", A handout created and distributed by Hope Church where Craig is Pastor for Adult Discipleship, Mason, OH, 21 March, 2018.

55. Bob and Joy Burney, "In Christ, We", (Westerville, OH: CrossPower Ministries, 2004).

56. John Piper, "The Stupendous Reality of Being in Christ Jesus", © Desiring God Foundation. Source: desiringGod.org, (https://www.desiringgod.org/articles/the-stupendous-reality-of-being-in-christ-jesus).

57. Susan Borgstrom, taken from *Journaling in Nature–a guided journal*, (http://www.lifepathcoach.net). Blog URL. (Susan developed this resource specifically for *Soul Nourishment*.)

58. Bill Gaultiere, (http://www.soulshepherding.org/2003/07/gods-love-letter-to-you/), 02 April 2018. Blog URL.

Thoughts on the SOUL

Nourishing it, being intentional about it, pursuing its nourishment, and listening to the soul

Thoughts on Spiritual Practices & Disciplines

Prayer, Scripture, Solitude and Silence

My Soul Check-up

How did I do?

My Response to 130 Ways to Draw Close to God

What are my top 5 choices?

My Ideas for Spending Time with God and Connecting to Him

My Journaling Practice